JARROLD SHORT WALKS
leisure walks for all ages

the New Forest National Park

Compiled by
David Foster

D1426056

JARROLD
publishing

Mapping sourced from **OS** Ordnance Survey®

Acknowledgements
I am grateful to Ian Lawrence of Hampshire County Council; to the Forestry Commission for confirming access arrangements; and to Tourist Information Centres and the Local Studies section at Winchester Library. I also owe a huge debt of gratitude to Mike Read, for his knowledge of the New Forest and its wildlife.

Text:	David Foster
Photography:	Mike Read and David Foster
Editorial:	Ark Creative (UK) Ltd.
Design:	Ark Creative (UK) Ltd.

While every care has been taken to ensure the accuracy of the route directions, the publishers cannot accept responsibility for errors or omissions, or for changes in details given. The countryside is not static: hedges and fences can be removed, field boundaries can be altered, footpaths can be rerouted and changes in ownership can result in the closure or diversion of some concessionary paths. Also, paths that are easy and pleasant for walking in fine conditions may become slippery, muddy and difficult in wet weather, while stepping stones across rivers and streams may become impassable.

If you find an inaccuracy in either the text or maps, please write to Crimson Publishing at the address below.

First published 2003 by Jarrold Publishing. Revised and reprinted 2005, 2007

This edition first published in Great Britain 2008 by Crimson Publishing, a division of:
Crimson Business Ltd
Westminster House, Kew Road
Richmond, Surrey, TW9 2ND
www.totalwalking.co.uk

Printed in Singapore. 5/08

Front cover: Alamy (Stock Image/Pixland)
Previous page: Autumnal colours in Berry wood

Contents

Keymap

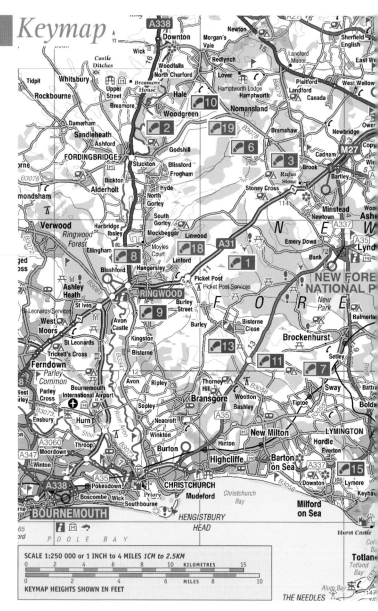

SCALE 1:250 000 or 1 INCH to 4 MILES *1CM to 2.5KM*

0   2   4   6   8   10   KILOMETRES   15

0   2   4   6   MILES   8   10

KEYMAP HEIGHTS SHOWN IN FEET

Introduction

The light was failing in the woods as I plodded up the valley at the end of a long day's walking. At dusk, these ancient woodlands cling tight, and the trees huddle round for the night. A little tired, I sat down to rest on a fallen log: a deer scuttered off through the trees and the woods fell silent. A short time later, I broke clear of the trees and stepped out onto a wide heath in the last of the evening sunshine. It was as if some unseen film director had changed the location and turned up the lights. My mood lifted, and I covered the final mile with new enthusiasm.

A place apart

Arriving in the New Forest can give you a similar sensation: the place looks and feels so very different from the surrounding countryside that it's almost like going abroad.

That's not just an illusion. You will find around a tenth of all the world's lowland heaths in southern England – and of these, the New Forest's huge purple vistas are by far the largest and most important. Besides the heath, some 30,000 acres (12,140 ha) of woodland help the New Forest to live up to its name. Many of these woods have changed little since the end of the last Ice Age, and they are still managed for their wildlife and amenity value.

View over heathland, Burley Beacon

These are just some of the qualities that led to the designation of the New Forest National Park in 2005. The National Park Authority now has overall responsibility for planning, wildlife conservation and recreation within the Forest, but will work closely with the people and organisations that have made the Forest what it is today.

Origins

The English are funny about history. We still speak of New College, Oxford more than six centuries after it was founded – and the New Forest is a good deal older than that. The Saxon kings were already hunting in this part of Hampshire before the Norman Conquest. But in 1079, William I designated the New Forest as a royal hunting park, and introduced strict forest laws.

On pain of death, individual peasants were forbidden to enclose their crops, take timber for building, or catch game for their tables. Nevertheless, William granted them a number of rights that were held jointly (or in common). These people became known as 'commoners'; they could gather firewood or cut turf for fuel, and they were also allowed to pasture their animals on the open forest. This ancient system of commoning created the New Forest's characteristic landscape, and today's commoners still exercise similar rights. Over 5,000 of their grazing ponies and cattle help to maintain the familar heathland clearings.

The Forest at war

Over the centuries, the Crown's interest in the Forest turned from the sporting to the strategic. Large areas of woodland were 'inclosed' to provide timber for Royal Navy ships, many of which were built at Buckler's Hard on the nearby Beaulieu River. More recently, military airfields sprang up during the two World Wars. There was a bombing range at Ashley Walk, and Mulberry Harbours were constructed on the coast near Lepe in readiness for the Normandy landings in 1944.

Leisure

Today the pendulum has swung back, and up to 25 million people now use the New Forest every year for leisure and recreation. Walkers and cyclists can enjoy more than 100 miles (161km) of well-maintained off-road tracks, and there are plenty of places to stop for a cream tea, or a leisurely lunch in one of the Forest's traditional inns.

Rays of light in misty oakwood, Broomy Inclosure

Walking also mixes well with more formal attractions. Some of the routes in this book start from pretty country towns, and pass close to places like Beaulieu Abbey, and the St. Barbe Museum at Lymington.

Wildlife

The New Forest's woods and heaths, together with its significant areas of bog, are internationally important for wildlife. For instance, the New Forest is a significant stronghold for the attractive little Dartford warbler, which is limited to lowland heaths, and the delicate wild gladiolus occurs nowhere else in Britain.

All six British reptile species are found on the heath, including harmless lizards and snakes. Adders live here too, their distinctive dark brown zigzag markings setting them apart as Britain's only poisonous snakes. But do not let them put you off your walk: adders rarely attack humans, and you are far more likely to be killed by a bee or a wasp sting.

Of course, you will see plenty of the New Forest's famous ponies on most of your walks. Dogs can be a potential problem near grazing animals, but they also pose a threat to birds that nest on the ground or in low scrub. Please keep your dog under close control to avoid disturbing them, especially during the nesting season from March to July.

Setting off

Except on the major roads, there is a maximum speed limit of 40mph throughout the New Forest. Do please drive safely within the limit – many ponies and other animals are killed every year as they wander in front of speeding cars. Incidentally, despite their placid appearance ponies can be aggressive, so it is wisest to watch them from a safe distance.

Most of the walks in this book offer easy route finding, and some even have good, all-weather surfaces. But you will also find a few references to busy road crossings, as well as indistinct forest paths and trackless heaths, where you will need good weather and a degree of care. On these routes, a small GPS receiver can help you to make the most of the information in these pages.

It is also worth taking a pair of binoculars and a good field guide with you on your walks. The route descriptions highlight particular things to look out for, and you will be surprised at how many different plants, animals and insects you can spot.

I had a wonderful time preparing these routes. If you get half as much pleasure from them as I did, then I can promise you some pretty enjoyable days out in the New Forest.

With the introduction of **'gps enabled' walks**, you will see that this book now includes a list of waypoints alongside the description of the walk. We have included these so that you can enjoy the full benefits of gps should you wish to. Gps is an amazingly useful and entertaining navigational aid, and you do not need to be computer literate to enjoy it.

GPS waypoint co-ordinates add value to your walk. You will now have the extra advantage of introducing 'direction' into your walking which will enhance your leisure walking and make it safer. Use of a gps brings greater confidence and security and you will find you cover ground a lot faster should you need to.

For more detailed information on using your gps, a *Pathfinder Guide* introducing you to gps and digital mapping is now available. *GPS for Walkers*, written by experienced gps teacher and navigation trainer Clive Thomas, is available in bookshops (ISBN 978-0-7117-4445-5) or order online at www.totalwalking.co.uk

● Pleasant views ● fallow deer ● woodland scents ● memorial stone

1 *Bolderwood deer sanctuary*

With its views across open heathland, this charming woodland walk is an ideal introduction to the New Forest. Go quietly along the easily graded tracks, and you'll probably see ponies and the occasional deer. Several benches along the route tempt you to bring a picnic and, near the end, you will pass the attractive Radnor Stone.

START Bolderwood Green
DISTANCE 2 miles (3.3km)
TIME 1 hour
PARKING Large Forestry Commission car park at start (suggested donation £2)
ROUTE FEATURES Easy navigation and walking, with one short, moderate climb near the end. The route is suitable for all-terrain buggies, but not recommended for wheelchair users. Dogs must be led

Head out onto the road near the toilet building. Now turn left, and follow the roadside verge past the Ornamental Drive, which branches off on your left towards Bolderwood Arboretum. Continue as far as the twin white flagpoles of the Canadian Memorial on your right.

A Swing hard left onto the gravel track opposite the memorial, and carry on past the 'Burley 5 miles' waymark post and a wooden barrier. Settle into your stride as the track drops gently down through dappled shade, with

pleasant views towards Bratley Inclosure on your right. Gradually the track becomes more wooded, and you'll start to enjoy the sweetly scented atmosphere of the mixed

> You'll often see fallow deer in the field below the viewing platform, and it's worth bringing your binoculars to watch them close up. They are the most common deer in the **New Forest**, though you may occasionally see other species as well. The name 'fallow' comes from the Old English falu, or 'spotted', and refers to the deer's dappled summer coat. The males grow fresh antlers every year, shedding their old ones in the spring.

PUBLIC TRANSPORT None
REFRESHMENTS Ice cream and cold drinks caravan usually parked at the start
PUBLIC TOILETS At the start
PICNIC/PLAY AREA Forestry Commission picnic area at the start
ORDNANCE SURVEY MAPS Explorer OL22 (New Forest)

conifer woodland. Pass the deer sanctuary at Bolderwood Farm on your left, cross a cattle-grid, and continue down the slope for a further 350 yds (320m).

B Turn left onto a gravel track marked by a red-banded wooden post. Follow this track for almost 300 yds (274m). Then, as it bends sharply right, turn left onto a narrower track between two more red-banded waymark posts. A few paces farther on, keep left at the

The Radnor Stone, Bolderwood

GPS WAYPOINTS

🖉 SU 243 086		**B** SU 235 080
A SU 239 092		**C** SU 240 083

? *How old is the Canadian Memorial?*

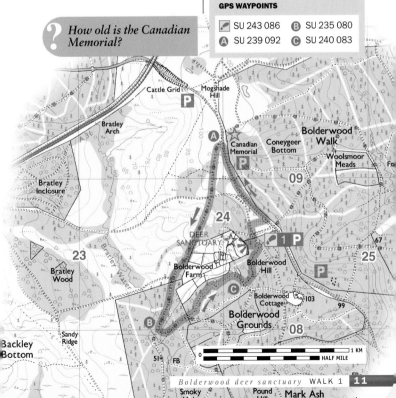

fork, where the waymark post is banded with red and green.

The buildings and fields of Bolderwood Farm are now on your left, and here the path leads you through the Bolderwood Arboretum. On this section you'll pass a fallen tree on your right, with strange, unearthly roots. Some 50 yds (46m) farther on, the track forks at a red and green waymark post close to an old, silted-up pond.

C Fork right, and continue for 100 yds (91m) to a junction marked by a red and green waymark post and a wooden bench

The Canadian Memorial is one of two wartime landmarks in the area. A mile and a half (2.4km) along the road towards **Emery Down**, the Portuguese Fireplace marks the site of a First World War camp. The camp was home to a Portuguese army unit that worked alongside local people, producing timber for the war effort. The fireplace was part of the cookhouse, and now stands as a memorial to the men who lived and worked here.

seat. Turn left here up the narrower gravel path, and soon you'll reach the beautifully carved Radnor Stone, just off the path to your right. The stone was erected in memory of the seventh Earl of Radnor, a former New Forest Verderer and chairman of the Forestry Commission.

Continue past the Radnor Stone, and soon you'll spot the deer viewing platform through the trees on your left. Just before the path crosses the Ornamental Drive, a signpost points your way along a gravel track towards the platform – although the wording is only visible after you've passed it! Turn left here for the short walk to the platform itself.

Now you can glimpse the car park through the trees on your right, and an easy stroll takes you back across the Ornamental Drive to your car. ●

Bolderwood deer sanctuary

Godshill Ridge

2

START Ashley Walk, on B3078, ¾ mile (1.2km) east of Godshill

DISTANCE 2 miles (3.2km)

TIME 1 hour

PARKING Forestry Commission car park at start

ROUTE FEATURES Mostly easy walking, but with one short, steep descent. May be slippery or muddy in places after rain

This pleasant rural walk contrasts brisk, open heathland with an intimate stroll along a quiet farm trackway. You can enjoy some good views across the New Forest, stop for a break in the village pub, and even visit Godshill Pottery for a locally made souvenir.

Cross the road from the car park to a low wooden barrier, and join the grassy track that runs at right angles to the road. Keep the wire fence on your left, and make your way through the heather and gorse, studded with holly and young silver birch.

Soon the track drops steeply down, and there are fine views across Millersford Bottom towards Godshill Inclosure. The Millersford brook runs into the River Avon near the 13th-century manor of Folds Farm, where there may once have been a mill on the

Sign at the Fighting Cocks public house, Godshill

PUBLIC TRANSPORT Limited service from Fordingbridge (0870 608 2608)

REFRESHMENTS The Fighting Cocks, Godshill

PUBLIC TOILETS None

PICNIC/PLAY AREA Godshill Ridge is a pleasant spot for informal picnics

ORDNANCE SURVEY MAPS Explorer OL22 (New Forest)

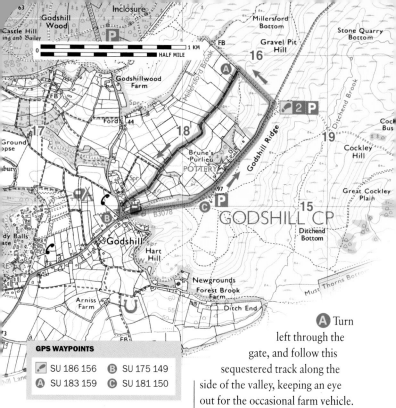

GPS WAYPOINTS

✏ SU 186 156   Ⓑ SU 175 149
Ⓐ SU 183 159   Ⓒ SU 181 150

site of the modern farmhouse. There are also fords across the brook a little farther down the valley.

Go carefully as you make your way down the bank, which can be slippery in wet weather. The slope eases off as you approach an area of thick bracken – keep a sharp look-out here for a metal gate, hiding in the trees on your left, with a blue waymark arrow on the gatepost. It's easy to miss it.

Ⓐ Turn left through the gate, and follow this sequestered track along the side of the valley, keeping an eye out for the occasional farm vehicle. Continue through a second metal gate, and follow the path as it climbs briefly through a double bend; this section can be muddy at times. The area, known as Brune's Purlieu, was owned by the Brune family for five centuries.

You can often see fallow and occasional red deer grazing in these fields around dusk, and a walk at this time will bring you to the Fighting Cocks pub in time for an evening drink. As you approach

? *Who laid the foundation stone of Godshill Village Hall, and when?*

Godshill village you pass the rustic garden gate at Cob Cottage, and at length the path leads you out opposite the village hall.

B Turn left past the Fighting Cocks, which takes its name from the old cockfighting pit on the common, then turn left again onto the B3078. Cross over here, and follow the road up onto Godshill Ridge. But do not take this too literally – there is plenty of open heathland on the right, and you can pick an attractive route through the bushes and up to the summit at Godshill cricket pitch.

There's a timeless atmosphere at the charming little **Godshill Pottery**, which seems to have taken root in Chris and Kate Charman's garden without anyone really noticing. The family has lived here since Chris's grandfather built the house in 1914 – now, Chris and Kate display their range of hand-made pottery and greetings cards in a compact huddle of outbuildings. The pottery is open until 5pm Monday to Saturday, but closes 1pm – 2pm for lunch. There are no refreshment or toilet facilities.

C *To visit Godshill Pottery, cross the road here and follow the verge for 100 yds (91m) to the pottery gate.* Afterwards, simply cross back onto the right-hand side of the road and complete the walk back to your car. ●

New Forest pony foal, Godshill

3 *Facts and fancies at Rufus Stone*

Starting with a leisurely stroll through native woodland, the route soon reaches the hamlet of Lower Canterton. Here, a bridleway carries you between luxuriant hedgerows to join the quiet lane that leads past the Sir Walter Tyrrell Inn and back to the Rufus Stone.

START Rufus Stone (1½ miles [2.4km] west of M27 junction 1)

DISTANCE 1½ miles (2.4km)

TIME 1 hour

PARKING Small Forestry Commission car park at Rufus Stone

ROUTE FEATURES Easy walking with gentle slopes, muddy in places any time of year. Dogs should be led near houses at Lower Canterton

A three-sided cast iron pillar now stands over the original Rufus Stone, which marks a turning point in British history. King William II was out hunting here in August 1100 when he was hit and killed by a stray arrow from Sir Walter Tyrrell's bow. Was his death really an accident? Historians have argued about that, but the King's body was laid in a cart and taken for burial in Winchester's great Norman cathedral, which had been completed just seven years earlier.

Nuthatch

? *Why is the monument to King William II called the Rufus Stone?*

PUBLIC TRANSPORT Irregular buses from Southampton and Lyndhurst to Castle Malwood ½ mile (800m) from the start (0870 608 2608)

REFRESHMENTS Sir Walter Tyrrell Inn

PUBLIC TOILETS None

PICNIC/PLAY AREA Play area at the pub

ORDNANCE SURVEY MAPS Explorer OL22 (New Forest)

From the car park opposite the Rufus Stone, set off into the trees at right angles to the road, leaving the cottage access on your left. The oak, beech and holly trees stand shy of the woodland path as it drops down to a tiny ford paved with concrete 'sandbags'. Jump across, leaving the fenced fields of Malwood Farm on your right, and take the left-hand fork. From here it's an easy walk through the woods to the broad clearing at Greys Farm.

C S Lewis, who wrote the seven children's books in the *Chronicles of Narnia* series, came to Hampshire on holiday in 1933. It's known that he went for a walk in these woods, and they

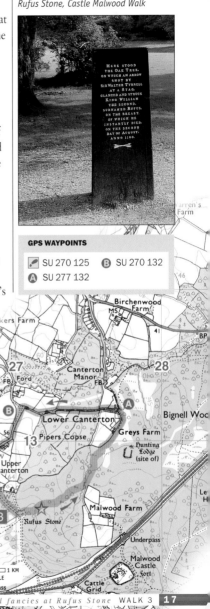

Rufus Stone, Castle Malwood Walk

HERE STOOD
THE OAK TREE,
ON WHICH AN ARROW
SHOT BY
Sir WALTER TYRRELL
AT A STAG,
GLANCED AND STRUCK
KING WILLIAM
THE SECOND,
SURNAMED RUFUS,
ON THE BREAST,
OF WHICH HE
INSTANTLY DIED,
ON THE SECOND
DAY OF AUGUST,
ANNO 1100.

GPS WAYPOINTS

SU 270 125 **B** SU 270 132
A SU 277 132

Sir Walter Tyrrell public house, Upper Canterton

may have inspired the Wood Between the Worlds, which Lewis described in *The Magician's Nephew* more than 20 years later.

Bear left across the green, join the gravelled track that leads past the tile-hung Greys Farm, and bear left

> All kinds of legends grew up after King William's death. Sir Walter Tyrrell's arrow bounced off an oak tree, and killed the King where the **Rufus Stone** now stands. According to tradition, the tree miraculously came into bud every year on Christmas Day, and a ghostly procession is said to follow William's funeral route ...
>
> Fleeing from the scene, Sir Walter is reputed to have stopped to have his horse's shoes refitted – backwards – to confuse his pursuers.

past Langley Cottage to a turning on your left.

A Turn left onto the signposted bridleway at 'Woodpeckers', and follow it through the woods until it joins a tarred lane at a second bridleway signpost. Continue along this narrow lane between tumbling hedges of dog rose, honeysuckle and hawthorn, as far as the T-junction and letterbox.

B Turn left at the junction, and follow the roadside verge past the attractive Canterton Manor Farm to the Sir Walter Tyrrell Inn. The pub is pleasantly situated looking out over a wide lawn; from here, it's just a short stroll back up the gentle rise to your car. ●

Shatterford and Bishop's Dyke

4

START On the B3056, just west of Beaulieu Road Station
DISTANCE 2½ miles (4km)
TIME 1½ hours
PARKING Small Forestry Commission car park at Shatterford
ROUTE FEATURES Easy walk on heath and forest edge tracks, with one short, trackless section through Denny Wood. Please keep dogs under close control

This charming walk encompasses the three main elements of the New Forest – heath, woodland and bog. Nevertheless, you're unlikely to get wet feet, as the route crosses the damper areas on footbridges and well-built causeways. Besides the inevitable ponies, you might see dragonflies, fallow deer, and even the occasional sand lizard.

Leave the car park at a low wooden barrier and head out over the open heathland, parallel to the railway line. Half a mile farther on, the track bears to the right over a gravel causeway and wooden footbridge, and parts company from the railway. Continue along the sandy track and follow it over two footbridges, close to some attractive pools fringed with silver birch.

A One hundred yards (91m) beyond the second bridge, the track splits into two at the edge of the woods. Take the narrower right-hand fork, close to a big oak tree, and continue through the trees into a large clearing. Fork right again, and then follow the

Pair of small red damselfly

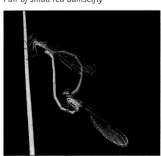

PUBLIC TRANSPORT Trains to Beaulieu Road Station (08457 48 49 50)
REFRESHMENTS Beaulieu Road Inn
PUBLIC TOILETS None
PICNIC/PLAY AREA None, but plenty of attractive spots for informal picnics along the route
ORDNANCE SURVEY MAPS Explorer OL22 (New Forest)

GPS WAYPOINTS

SU 348 063   **B** SU 335 053

A SU 345 050   **C** SU 339 058

edge of Denny Lodge Inclosure on your left.

The track wanders along outside the woods, sometimes with heathland on your right, sometimes with trees on both sides. Continue across two small footbridges as the track bears right, away from the woods. Three more bridges bring you to Denny Wood,

> This area is well known for **birdwatching**. You may see stonechats or Dartford warblers, which nest in low scrub, as well as ground-nesting birds like woodlark or nightjar. To avoid disturbing them, please keep your dog under close control, especially between March and July when the birds are nesting.

where you can just make out the faint earthworks of the Bishop's Dyke near the edge of the wood.

The dyke probably dates from prehistoric times, but an old guide to the New Forest recounts a more entertaining tradition. According to this version, a playful monarch offered to grant the Bishop of Winchester all the land that he could crawl around in a day.

If the story seems far-fetched, there's a striking parallel with one of Hampshire's oldest traditions, the Tichborne Dole. In honour of Lady Tichborne's dying wish, a measure of flour is still 'doled out' to local parishioners once a year – but the bequest was hard-won. Lord Tichborne dedicated all the corn his wife could crawl around while a torch was burning and, to this day, these fields are known as The Crawls.

B Follow the path into the woods and turn right. Keeping the Bishop's Dyke on your right, pick your way along the trackless woodland edge for about 200 yds (182m). Here you'll find a rough woodland path, about 50 yds (46m) inside the woods. Continue along this path – always keeping the woodland edge in sight – and turn north at the corner of the woods where the path begins to climb.

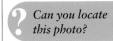

Traffic on the major routes west of Southampton frequently grinds to a halt at weekends in summer, and trying to park in any of the popular centres isn't the best way to begin a day in the country. But you don't have to get caught up in all that; jump on the train, and follow this delightful route from **Beaulieu Road Station**.

C Now the path levels off and breaks clear of Denny Wood, giving you a wide view across the heather and bracken to the buildings at Beaulieu Road Station. Turn right here onto a grassy track that strikes across the heath, heading a few degrees to the left of the station buildings. The path winds confidently through the heather, crossing the boggy Shatterford Bottom on a gravel causeway and footbridge as it carries you back to your car. ●

Can you locate this photo?

5 *Hatchet Pond*

This gentle walk includes a variety of typical New Forest scenery, with opportunities to picnic beside the popular Hatchet Pond. The route creates a sense of isolation, but the navigation is straightforward and you're never far from civilisation.

START Top of Furzey Lane, near Hatchet Gate

DISTANCE 2¾ miles (4.5km)

TIME 1½ hours

PARKING Small Forestry Commission car park at Rans Wood

ROUTE FEATURES Varied walking that includes some poorly defined paths through the heather. Long, easy slopes, but with some muddy areas after rain

Start from the low wooden barrier and follow the off-road cycle route out of the car park, waymarked towards Brockenhurst. The track winds briefly through the woods, and emerges onto a rough, gorse-studded heath. Follow the cycle route until it dives into Hawk-hill Inclosure at a five-bar gate.

Ⓐ Leave the track here, and turn left onto the grassy path along the edge of the woods. The path negotiates several boggy areas on little causeway bridges, and there's a pleasant view out over the heathland on your left. Besides the heather and gorse, look out for low-growing bog myrtle with its woody stems.

Hatchet Pond was created around 1790, and the main road from Beaulieu to Lymington was routed over the causeway. The water originally flowed through a leat under the road and powered the low-lying **Hatchet Mill**, which was served by an overshot water wheel. The milling machinery has now been removed, and the house is privately owned.

PUBLIC TRANSPORT Buses to Hatchet Gate from Lymington and Hythe (0870 608 2608)

REFRESHMENTS An ice cream van is often parked near the car park entrance at Hatchet Pond

PUBLIC TOILETS At Hatchet Pond car park

PICNIC/PLAY AREA Bench seats at Hatchet Pond

ORDNANCE SURVEY MAPS Explorer OL22 (New Forest)

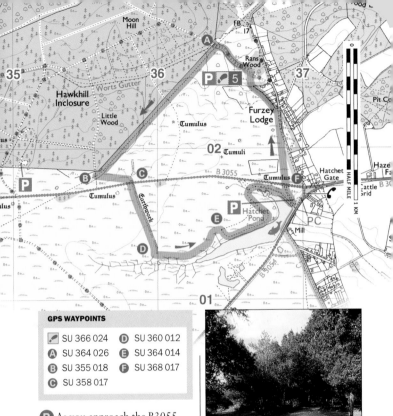

GPS WAYPOINTS

🖊 SU 366 024	Ⓓ SU 360 012
Ⓐ SU 364 026	Ⓔ SU 364 014
Ⓑ SU 355 018	Ⓕ SU 368 017
Ⓒ SU 358 017	

Ⓑ As you approach the B3055 road, the woods peel away to the right; double back here onto a rough path on your left, heading just to the left of a clump of pine trees on the near horizon. The path converges with the road close to a gorse-capped ancient earthwork.

Ⓒ Cross over, and join a narrow path through the heather, parallel with the earthwork's bank and ditch 10 yds (9m) on your left. The path gradually improves until, after

Rans Wood, near Furzey Lodge

about 550 yds (503m), you'll come to a low depression in the heath, marked by a wet, boggy area.

Ⓓ Do not get your boots wet here, but turn off to the left onto a more substantial gravel track, heading for

Hatchet Pond

Fawley power station's tall concrete chimney poking above the trees on the far horizon. Soon the wide expanse of Hatchet Pond opens up on your right, and a track branches off towards the water.

E Turn right, and follow the track as it curves left along the water's edge. As the shoreline bends to the left, the path splits into two; fork right, a stone's throw from the shore, and continue bearing right through the trees that guard the pond's boggy northern arm. Beyond the trees, keep going beside the water until you reach the car park access road; turn left, and cross the B3055.

F Keep straight on across the heath, gradually converging with Furzey Lane near the low, cream-painted bungalow at Forest End. In

? *What is the local meaning of the word 'hatchet'?*

dry weather, the nicest route veers off to the left here, and you can pick your way around the back of the houses for the last 300 yds (274m) back to the car park. However, this section can be quite muddy after rain so, if you prefer, simply use the road to complete your walk. ●

During your walk, you'll probably notice model aircraft in the skies over **Hatchet Moor**. Enthusiasts now fly their models from the site of **Beaulieu** airfield, which was opened by the RAF in August 1942. Initially, this big, three runway airfield was used by RAF Coastal Command and the RCAF to fly anti U-boat missions. Later, US Air Force planes arrived to support the D-Day landings in 1944. The base was closed in 1950.

Fritham

START Eyeworth Pond, Fritham

DISTANCE 2½ miles (4.3km)

TIME 1½ hours

PARKING Small Forestry Commission car park at the start

ROUTE FEATURES Long, gentle slopes and good tracks, but with one short boggy section. Dogs should be led near grazing animals

6

The charming old Royal Oak – once known as the Parliament of the New Forest – lies at the heart of unspoilt Fritham. This route climbs steadily up the valley from Eyeworth Pond, and there are attractive views on the return over Longcross Plain.

Turn right out of the car park, pass a wooden barrier, and continue up the gravel track with the pond just visible through the trees on your left.

Today, this area could scarcely be more peaceful. But, in the late 19th century, things were very different. A London businessman had founded a small gunpowder factory at Eyeworth Lodge in 1859 and, ten years later, the Schultze Gunpowder Company bought the firm out and began making powder for the Franco-German war.

Soon, the gently rising track pulls

The Royal Oak, Fritham

clear of the woods and enters an area of heath and low scrub. Just follow the track until, about 150 yds (137m) before it reaches the B3078, you'll see a rough path through the heather on your right.

A Turn off here, at right angles to

PUBLIC TRANSPORT Infrequent service from Southampton (0870 608 2608)

REFRESHMENTS The Royal Oak, Fritham

PUBLIC TOILETS None

PICNIC/PLAY AREA Plenty of informal picnic spots

ORDNANCE SURVEY MAPS Explorer OL22 (New Forest)

the track, and continue for 175 yds (160m) towards a low, compact gorse bush on the near horizon.

B *Here you have the option of visiting Longcross Pond. Cross the road near the triangular road sign and bear gently right through the heather for 330 yds (302m).* Otherwise turn right here, and join the grassy track that snakes away through the heather at about 45 degrees from the road.

C A few scattered trees mark your approach to Howen Bushes and the enclosed fields around Fritham. Keep ahead as the path dives into the woods; the rough woodland path is boggy at first, but it soon joins a farm track close to a field gate on your left. Continue along this track, passing a brick bungalow as you approach Fritham Green.

D *Here, you can divert for a few paces around the corner on your left to enjoy a drink at the Royal Oak.*

The name **Fritham** may come from the Old English 'fryhth', which meant the scrub on the edge of a forest, and 'hamm' – a cultivated plot in marginal land. These early descriptions reflect the modern village, surrounded by fields set in a landscape of heath and woodland.

Complete the walk by turning right past the restored Gunpowder Factory post box, and drop down the lane to your car at Eyeworth Pond. ●

? *What were the postal rates from the Gunpowder Factory postbox?*

GPS WAYPOINTS

SU 228 145	**C** SU 236 148
A SU 242 155	**D** SU 231 141
B SU 243 154	

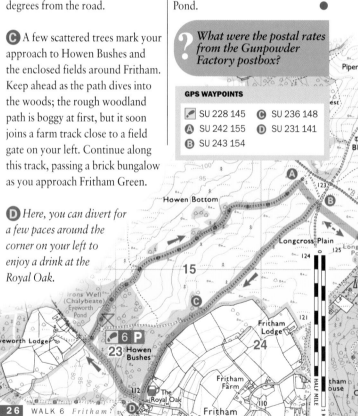

Setley Pond and Roydon Woods

START Setley Pond
DISTANCE 3 miles (4.8km)
TIME 1½ hours
PARKING Forestry Commission car park at the start
ROUTE FEATURES Several stiles at the start. Watch out for barbed wire in places. There are a couple of busy road crossings, and the route may be muddy. Please keep dogs on the lead near grazing animals, and in nature reserve

7

You have a choice of two pubs on this route, with the chance of some miniature boating at the end of the walk. Starting from Setley Pond, you'll follow country footpaths to Roydon Woods nature reserve. After winding your way through the ancient woodlands, the final section strikes out over the open heathland of Setley Plain.

Take the path to the right of the pond, bear around to the left, and cross a gravel road. Bear left again at Pinecroft, and continue for 100 yds (91m) on a grassy track. Now, look out for a stile tucked away off to your right – nip across, and follow the narrow path between hedges of holly, honeysuckle and young oak until you reach the A337 opposite The Hobler.

Ⓐ *Cross the road with care*, and turn left along the roadside pavement: then, just beyond the pub, turn right through a metal kissing-gate onto a signposted footpath. The waymarked path leads you over two stiles and through a couple of open fields, and there are some pleasant views across the little valley on your right.

Another stile and a wooden footbridge bring you to the start of a moderate slope. Tree-shaded at first, the path crosses two minor roads on its way to a kissing-gate at the entrance to Roydon Woods nature reserve.

PUBLIC TRANSPORT Southampton to Lymington buses stop at The Hobler (0870 608 2608)
REFRESHMENTS The Hobler and The Filly Inn
PUBLIC TOILETS None
PICNIC/PLAY AREA None
ORDNANCE SURVEY MAPS Explorer OL22 (New Forest)

? *What is the website address of the Hampshire & Isle of Wight Wildlife Trust?*

✚ The 218-ft high Peterson's tower on the **Arnewood Estate** was completed in the late-19th century after more than five years work. It's often dismissed as a folly, but the reinforced concrete building was ahead of its time and may have been an experiment in this new type of construction.

B Keep straight on to a four-way signpost, and dive into the woods at a five-bar gate. Most of the reserve is broadleaved woodland, with smaller areas of conifer plantations, meadows and heathland. The woods are a haven for butterflies, foxes, badgers and deer, as well as tawny owls and woodpeckers.

GPS WAYPOINTS

📄 SZ 302 992	**C**	SU 313 005
A SZ 306 990	**D**	SU 302 002
B SZ 313 995		

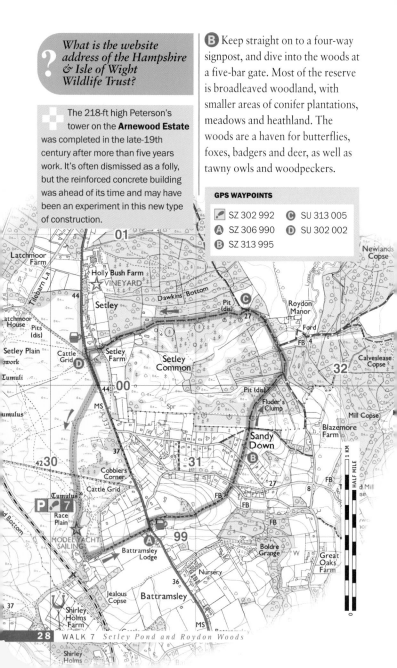

The bridleway drops gently over a small plank bridge to a T-junction with a gravel track, marked by a wooden signpost. Turn left here, and continue past a bridleway turning on the right. Then, follow the track as it bears left at The Lodge and climbs gently to a signposted fork.

C Keep left here, pass a small, disused quarry on your right, and carry on out of the reserve. As you approach the A337, you'll notice a number of driveways to woodland properties, so it's worth being alert for the occasional car. Just beyond the cattle-grid at the picturesque Setley Farm, pull up short at the busy main road junction. If you're ready for a break here, you'll find the Filly Inn just 50 yds (46m) up the verge on your right

D *Take great care as you cross the road*, and continue up the turning opposite, signposted to Sway. By-pass the cattle-grid, and turn immediately left onto a path through the gorse bushes, roughly parallel to the A337. After 200 yds (182m) it will lead you out onto a grazed area, studded with gorse and clumps of heather. Bear right here, heading just to the left of Peterson's tower on the skyline.

Continue across the heath, bearing gently to the left until you meet the road a few paces west of the entrance to Setley Pond car park. Cross over, and complete the last few yards back to your car. ●

Model yachting at Setley Pond

■ Colourful heaths ■ views ■ grazing animals ■ stream crossings

8 *Moyles Court*

START Just south of
Moyles Court School
DISTANCE 3 miles (4.8km)
TIME 2 hours
PARKING Roadside
parking for about 20 cars
on wide, gravelled verge
ROUTE FEATURES Several
stiles and some
moderate hills, with
short muddy sections at
any time of year. Poor
waymarking after leaving
the Avon Valley Path.
Dogs must be led near
grazing animals

*Starting from a shallow ford of the
Dockens Water, this route passes the
handsome 300-year-old Moyles Court
School and climbs steadily onto a heather-
clad plateau. There are grazing animals
here, as well as long views over the New
Forest. In early autumn the area is carpeted
with bright purple heather.*

Turn your back on the ford at
Dockens Water, and head up the
road towards Moyles Court
School. Some 130 yds (119m)
beyond the school entrance, turn

Dame Alice Lisle inherited
Moyles Court from her father.
After the battle of Sedgemoor in
1685, she gave shelter to three
fugitives from Monmouth's defeated
army. Alice was arrested the next day,
and taken for trial in Winchester. The
infamous Judge Jeffreys sentenced
her to be burned alive, although she
was actually beheaded after
petitioning James II. Her body was
returned to Ellingham, where she was
buried in St Mary's churchyard.

right through the metal kissing-
gate and follow the enclosed Avon
Valley Path around the edge of
gently rising paddocks. Views open
up as you skirt the edge of
Newlands Plantation; then, keep
straight on through the second
kissing-gate along a grassy path
through bracken and young birch
trees.

Now the route bears to the right
around a low hill, with views
towards Somerley Park across the
lakes behind you. More paddocks
open up on your left, and the Avon
Valley Path forks left at a stumpy

PUBLIC TRANSPORT Buses to Ellingham 1 mile (1.6km) (0870 608 2608)
REFRESHMENTS The Alice Lisle Inn, Rockford
PUBLIC TOILETS None
PICNIC/PLAY AREA Plenty of delightful spots for informal picnics
ORDNANCE SURVEY MAPS Explorer OL22 (New Forest)

30 WALK 8 *Moyles Court*

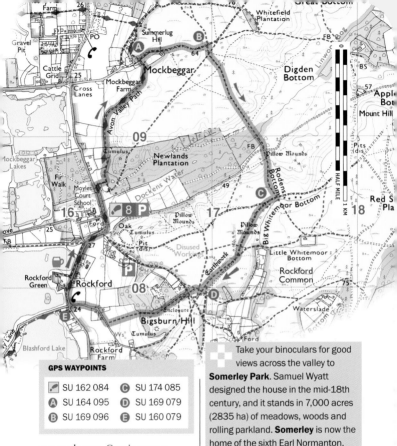

GPS WAYPOINTS

📝 SU 162 084		ⓒ SU 174 085	
Ⓐ SU 164 095		Ⓓ SU 169 079	
Ⓑ SU 169 096		Ⓔ SU 160 079	

waymark post. Continue to a signpost just before a large, red-roofed house; then, follow the path as it swings hard left over a narrow wooden causeway and up a steep bank to a rough gravel road.

Ⓐ Turn right onto this road, leaving the Avon Valley Path and climbing gently past a wooden barrier towards Summerlug Hill. The road gets narrower until, at a

Take your binoculars for good views across the valley to **Somerley Park**. Samuel Wyatt designed the house in the mid-18th century, and it stands in 7,000 acres (2835 ha) of meadows, woods and rolling parkland. **Somerley** is now the home of the sixth Earl Normanton, and has been in his family since 1825. The house is also used for conferences, but Somerley is never open to the public.

second barrier, it bears right onto a path through light woodland. Beyond the woods, the path levels off and opens into a wide heathland vista. Look out for a small pond just off the path on your left – a lovely picnic spot.

Pond at Summerlug Hill

B Directly opposite the pond, turn right onto a narrow path through the bracken. Continue south across the heath, with easy walking and glorious views. All too soon, the path dives steeply down towards the wooded valley, and crosses the Dockens Water on a metal-railed footbridge. It's often wet and muddy here.

Keep straight on across a minor road, and begin the short, stiff climb up through the heather. As the path levels off and starts to lose height, fork right. Then, after 50 yds (46m), turn right **C** onto a wider sandy track. Fork left after

? *Why are there so many lakes in the valley between Blashford and Ibsley?*

100 yds (91m) and follow the raised track past a broken wooden barrier, taking the wider gravel road as it dips across an open, gorse-covered area and climbs to a crossways.

D Turn right, and follow the track as it winds through the woods to the gate of Chatley Wood House. Turn left along the woodland path, keeping the grounds of the house on your right. The path drops to a stile and continues through an open field towards a second stile, just to the left of a prominent thatched cottage. Nip across, and turn right onto the back lane towards Rockford.

E Turn right at the crossroads towards Linwood. Beyond the Alice Lisle Inn, just across the green on your left, a stile leads onto the Avon Valley Path. A hedge separates you from the road on your right, and there are glimpses of Rockford Lake to your left. At the next stile, cross the turning to Ellingham and continue to the little green. Now, simply fork left across the Dockens Water and return to your car. ●

Ringwood

START Ringwood Tourist Information office

DISTANCE 4¼ miles (7km)

TIME 2 hours

PARKING Large Pay and Display car parks adjacent to the Furlong shopping precinct

ROUTE FEATURES Level walking with easy access from the town centre, but with numerous stiles. The riverside sections include some damp meadows, which may flood at any time of year

9

The walk follows the Avon Valley Path as it weaves its way out of Ringwood and heads south through tranquil water meadows towards Christchurch. Looping back through farmland and along country lanes, you can visit Liberty's Raptor and Reptile Centre before approaching Ringwood via its old railway line and the green acres of Bickerley Common.

Cross the road from the tourist information centre, and follow the Avon Valley Path down Meeting House Lane. Bear right into Market Place, and continue past the church into West Street. Cross the Mill Stream bridge, and turn immediately left.

Now the path leads you through a small mobile home park to a

? *What's so special about the large lamp standard in Ringwood Market Place?*

kissing-gate, before bearing left through a field to re-cross the river on a waymarked footbridge. Continue through an area of attractive housing at Bickerley Common, bearing right again at the big Avon Valley Path signpost to cross the river and old railway line.

A Cross the stile in the old railway fence and bear right along the Avon Valley Path, crossing the narrow wooden causeway as you head for the stile on the far side of the field. Turn left after the stile (dogs on leads here, please) and

PUBLIC TRANSPORT Buses from all major centres (0870 608 2608)

REFRESHMENTS Plenty of pubs and cafés in Ringwood; café at Liberty's Raptor & Reptile Centre

PUBLIC TOILETS At the start

PICNIC/PLAY AREA None

ORDNANCE SURVEY MAPS Explorer OL22 (New Forest)

Kingfisher, Avon

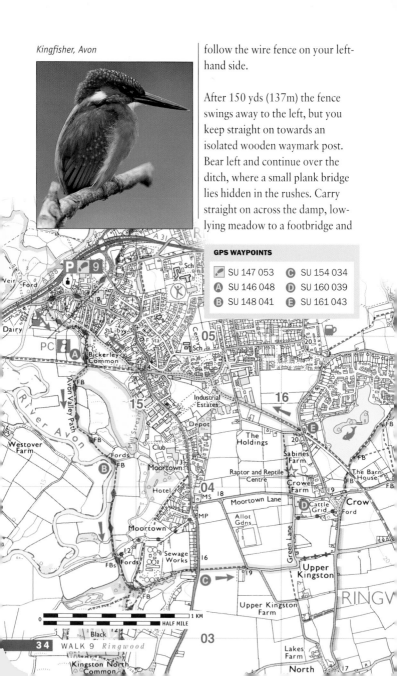

follow the wire fence on your left-hand side.

After 150 yds (137m) the fence swings away to the left, but you keep straight on towards an isolated wooden waymark post. Bear left and continue over the ditch, where a small plank bridge lies hidden in the rushes. Carry straight on across the damp, low-lying meadow to a footbridge and

GPS WAYPOINTS

SU 147 053	Ⓒ SU 154 034
Ⓐ SU 146 048	Ⓓ SU 160 039
Ⓑ SU 148 041	Ⓔ SU 161 043

two stiles, as the path draws alongside the broad, smooth-flowing River Avon on your right.

B Bear right, briefly following the river before the path bears away gently to the left, crosses a stile, and runs between thick hedges 30 yds (27m) from the river bank. A lazy walk amid dog rose and willow-herb brings you to a shallow ford and three footbridges – once safely across, continue along the Avon Valley Path, still walking in the same direction.

Cross the cattle-grid and continue for 100 yds (91m) to a signpost, where the Avon Valley Path bears away to the right. Turn left down the footpath between two houses – Oaklands and Lake View – and follow the gravel track, looking out for glimpses of the lake through the trees on your right. Pass a pretty thatched cottage on your left before reaching the B3347 at Jessamine Cottage.

C Cross over, and take the footpath straight across the open field towards a slate-roofed house, where the path emerges onto a back road. Bear right onto the road; then, after 100 yds (91m), fork left into Green Lane and follow it through to the junction with

Walking near Ringwood

Moortown Lane.

D *To visit the Raptor and Reptile Centre, turn right for the short diversion along Moortown Lane, then left at the crossroads; the Centre is a further 200 yds (182m) on your left. After your visit, turn left out of the Centre to rejoin the walk at point* **E**.

C For the main route, turn left for 20 yds (18m) to the stile on your right. Jump over, and follow the

The **Avon** valley includes a wider range of wildlife habitats than any other similar area in Britain. Its fens, mires, small woods and extensive traditional hay meadows are home to large numbers of wetland birds and breeding waders. The floodplain is also an essential safety valve for the river itself, safeguarding local people from the worst effects of severe weather. Most of the valley is protected by national and European wildlife designations.

footpath beside the electric fence on your right, crossing another four stiles to Crow Arch Lane. Turn right; then, a few paces short of the next road junction, turn sharp left **E** through the wooden kissing-gate onto a footpath along the old railway line.

Continue under a brick arch bridge and over a stile into a small industrial estate on the site of Ringwood's old railway station. Embankment Way leads you through the estate to the junction with Castleman Way, named after Charles Castleman, promoter of the Southampton and Dorchester Railway, which closed in 1964. Turn left, and follow Castleman Way through to a mini roundabout. There is a pavement on the left but,

Just over halfway around your walk, a short diversion along minor roads will bring you to **Liberty's Raptor and Reptile Centre** (01425 476487). Liberty's is home to a large collection of eagles, hawks, owls and vultures, as well as snakes, lizards and tortoises. There are daily flying displays, with other events at weekends and holidays. There are also a gift shop, café and toilets. Allow at least two hours for your visit.

for a nicer walk, cross over at Waterloo Way and use the landscaped footway as far as the Railway Hotel.

Keep straight on at the roundabout, and follow Bickerley Road up the side of Bickerley Common to rejoin the Avon Valley Path and retrace your outward steps back to the car park. ●

Yellow iris beside the River Avon

Hale Park and Woodgreen

10

START Hale Purlieu

DISTANCE 4 miles (6.2km)

TIME 2 hours

PARKING Small National Trust car park at start

ROUTE FEATURES There are several stiles along this undulating easy-to-follow walk, and some sections may be muddy. An uphill stretch leads back to the main route if you divert to the pub

After skirting the heaths of Hale Purlieu, the route winds along a charming rhododendron-fringed bridleway to Hatchet Green. From here, it follows the Avon Valley path past the imposing Georgian mansion of Hale House as far as the scattered rural community of Woodgreen. The return, across fields and along a shady trackway, ends with a heathland finale.

With your back to the car park entrance, walk past the low wooden barriers and bear left through the trees onto a grassy path through the bracken. This quickly leads to the edge of an open heath; turn left along the narrow, stony path, roughly parallel with the woodland edge.

Turn left at the unmarked crossways directly beneath the power lines, and return to the road. Cross over, go through the metal gate, and join the waymarked byway as it veers right along a grassy path through the trees. After 220 yds (201m) turn right onto a bridleway at the signposted crossways. This pleasant, shady track winds between rhododendron bushes and mature trees to end at a gate leading out onto a tarred lane.

A Turn left along the lane for 65 yds (59m); then, as it bends to the right, fork left onto a gravelled track for the short stretch to Hale village hall and Hatchet Green. Turn left along the edge of the green, past the Millennium statue, and then bear right to the

PUBLIC TRANSPORT Limited service from Fordingbridge to Hale and Woodgreen (0870 608 2608)

REFRESHMENTS The Horse and Groom, Woodgreen

PUBLIC TOILETS None

PICNIC/PLAY AREA None

ORDNANCE SURVEY MAPS Explorer OL22 (New Forest)

? *Who sculpted the Millennium Statue at Hatchet Green?*

T-junction at the Old Post Office. Now turn left along the lane, joining the route of the Avon Valley Path, and follow it for just over ½ mile (800m) until the lane bends left at Home Farm. Continue for a further 60 yds (55m).

B Turn right towards St Mary's church, still following the signposted Avon Valley Path beside the impressive tree-lined drive to Hale House. Cross a track that sweeps in from the right; then, as you approach the house, bear right onto the narrow woodland

footpath that drops past St Mary's church to a junction with Moot Lane.

The manor of Hale dates back to at least 1538, when it was bought by the Penruddocke family. After nearly two centuries the family sold the estate to London architect Thomas Archer, who demolished the Elizabethan manor house and replaced it with the Georgian building that stands to this day.

GPS WAYPOINTS

SU 188 177	**D** SU 175 176
A SU 194 189	**E** SU 180 177
B SU 183 187	**F** SU 187 175
C SU 177 186	

C Turn left, following the Avon Valley Path along the lane, with glimpses of the river through the trees on your right. Bear right at the road junction towards Woodgreen and Breamore; then, after 30 yds (27m), fork left up the drive to North End.

Fording the River Avon, Hale

A few paces bring you to a stile between two gates; nip across, and follow the grassy track along the right-hand edge of an open field. Three waymarked stiles lead you under the electricity lines and out onto a gravelled drive at Hollington. Keep straight on along the drive, following it as it bears left, climbs to a level section, and curves right to a junction marked by an Avon Valley Path signpost.

D *Keep straight on here if you fancy a break, then turn right onto the road for 400 yds (366m) to the Horse and Groom pub at the foot of the hill.*

Otherwise turn sharp left at the signpost, bear around to the right, and turn left over the stile between Fairburn and Logan Bank. The path drops down over a small plank bridge, then climbs to a waymarked kissing-gate and continues along the left-hand side of an open field. Halfway along the field, cross the waymarked stile on your left, and walk diagonally across the next field to a stile tucked into the corner, close to the entrance to Higherend Farm.

E Turn left; then, after a few paces, turn right along a tree-shaded track. Continue past a bridleway turning on your left until you reach the road at Hale Purlieu.

F Cross the road, turn left, and follow the woodland track that runs parallel with the road for the short way back to the car park. ●

During the latter half of the 13th century, the New Forest was extended to include the present day area of **Hale Pulieu**. But the arrangement lasted for little more than 20 years, after which the area was 'disafforested' and resumed its former status as a common. In 1964, nearly seven centuries later, Parliament returned Hale Purlieu to the New Forest.

11 Wilverley Inclosure

START Wilverley Inclosure

DISTANCE 4 miles (6.2km)

TIME 2 hours

PARKING Extensive Forestry Commission car park at the start (suggested donation £2)

ROUTE FEATURES Mainly easy walking on gravelled woodland tracks, but with a shallow ford across the Avon Water

This walk links two large areas of woodland. Starting from the wide grassy lawn of Wilverley Plain, you'll reach the Old Station Tea House on well-made tracks. Then, after fording the Avon Water, there's an easy return through the mixed woods and butterfly glades of Wootton Coppice Inclosure.

Leave the car park by the wooden gate at the start of the waymarked 'Wilverley Wander'. Bear right at the first junction, waymarked 'Scouts', and keep straight on at the bench seat 150 yds (137m) farther on. At this junction, look out for an interesting little Victorian cast iron marker plate on your left.

Follow the route marked with green and yellow banded posts until, in the heart of the Inclosure, the track bears left and drops to a crossways. Keep straight on here,

still following the green and yellow posts, and enjoying the birdsong and sweet forest scents. Now the track bears right, and climbs up to a steady, level section that brings you to a junction within earshot of the A35.

Ⓐ Swing hard left here along the waymarked cycle route. After a level start, the track winds downhill, then bears sharp left at a bench seat in memory of Josephine Collins. Fork right, leaving the gravelled route for a greener forest track. Continue straight over the forest

PUBLIC TRANSPORT Buses to Holmsley from Lyndhurst, Burley and Ringwood (0870 608 2608)

REFRESHMENTS Old Station Tea House, Holmsley

PUBLIC TOILETS At the start

PICNIC/PLAY AREA Forestry Commission picnic area at the start, and plenty of bench seats along the route in Wilverley Inclosure

ORDNANCE SURVEY MAPS Explorer OL22 (New Forest)

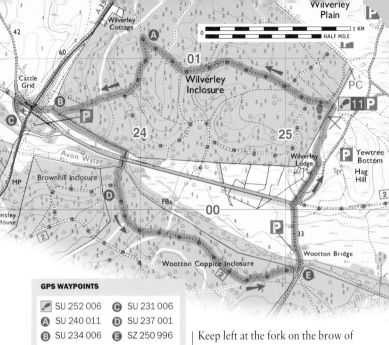

GPS WAYPOINTS

📎 SU 252 006	Ⓒ SU 231 006
Ⓐ SU 240 011	Ⓓ SU 237 001
Ⓑ SU 234 006	Ⓔ SZ 250 996

crossways after 120 yds (109m), and follow the track as it winds uphill through a conifer plantation.

Holmsley Station was the first stop after leaving Brockenhurst on the original railway from Southampton to Dorchester. When the line opened in 1847 coach services ran south to Christchurch, which did not get its own railway until 15 years later. The opening of the present main line through Bournemouth in 1888 signalled the steady decline of the 'Old Road' through Holmsley. After serving the nearby RAF airfield during the Second World War, the station saw its last train in 1964.

Keep left at the fork on the brow of the hill, and carry on through a belt of oak and holly before leaving the inclosure at a wooden five-bar gate. *You can skip tea by turning left here, and continue back to Wilverley – but you'll miss the point of the walk.*

Ⓑ Those who are serious about cream teas should turn right out of the woods. After 50 yds (46m) fork left, and continue past the line of concrete fence posts at the top of the old railway cutting. The path meanders down under the A35 bridge, where you'll glimpse your destination – the Old Station Tea House at Holmsley. Bear round to

Old Station Tea House, Holmsley

your left, then turn left at an electricity pole on the right and follow a pair of wires to the stile just across the road from the tea house.

C After tea, retrace your steps to point **B**. Follow the track along the woodland edge for 500 yds (457m), continuing onto a well-made gravel path that soon swings to the right and dives under the old railway bridge. Ford the Avon Water, and continue through a small wooden gate into Brownhill Inclosure. Now, a woodland path will lead you straight through to a gravelled forest track.

? *How large was Wilverley Inclosure in the 18th and 19th centuries?*

D Turn left, and follow this attractive, level route all the way through to Wootton Coppice Inclosure. You'll have a good mix of trees for company – everything from young birch and oak, through conifers to mature broadleaf trees.

E Leave Wootton Coppice Inclosure by a wooden gate, turn left onto the road, and cross Wootton Bridge. From the bridge, follow the rough path up the right-hand roadside verge, until it bears gently to the right and meets the road a few paces east of the junction. Cross over, and bear right onto the sandy track that runs parallel with the road up towards Wilverley Plain. Pass Wilverley Lodge, and continue across the drive to Wilverley Cottage. From here, it's just a short walk up the hill back to the car park. ●

You can still explore long sections of the old railway around **Holmsley**. Much of the line has been converted to walking and cycling routes, and Walk 13 includes an attractive length south of Burley. After the railway closed in 1964, Hampshire County Council re-routed more than a mile of the road from Burley to Lymington along the old trackbed east of Holmsley Station. This walk passes beneath the new roadway near Avon Water.

Lepe

12

START Lepe Country Park (beach car park)
DISTANCE 4½ miles (7.2km)
TIME 2½ hours
PARKING Large Pay and Display car park at the start
ROUTE FEATURES Undulating field and woodland paths, dotted with stiles, give way to a homeward walk along the beach

After a brief coastal section, the walk turns inland and makes its way north through a patchwork of field and woodland paths. An attractive farm road then leads you westwards for the cross-country tramp back to the coast. Finally, a bracing walk along the beach offers magnificent views out to the Isle of Wight.

Follow the coast road pavement from the car park, keeping the sea on your left. The saltings and mudflats along this section attract wading birds like oystercatcher and grey plover, and they are an important feeding area for Brent geese. Cross the Dark Water bridge and carry on along the gravel coast path as the road bears away to your right. Pass the white-painted Watch House, and continue as far as the lighthouse.

A Double back to the right, climb up onto the coast road, and turn left. About 140 yds (128m) farther on, you'll see a stile and wooden footpath signpost on your right. Nip across, and follow the field edge on your right, continuing as it bears left and through a field gate. Follow the rough track through the next field, and on through a second gate.

Now, with the wire fence on your right, continue over a stile. Keep straight on under the electricity

? *Can you guess the original purpose of Lepe's white-painted Watch House?*

PUBLIC TRANSPORT None
REFRESHMENTS Ice cream kiosk, licensed restaurant and shop at the start
PUBLIC TOILETS At the start
PICNIC/PLAY AREA None
ORDNANCE SURVEY MAPS Explorer OL22 (New Forest)

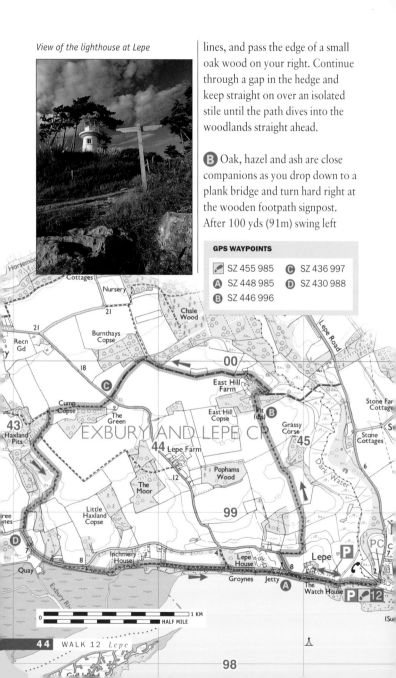

View of the lighthouse at Lepe

lines, and pass the edge of a small oak wood on your right. Continue through a gap in the hedge and keep straight on over an isolated stile until the path dives into the woodlands straight ahead.

B Oak, hazel and ash are close companions as you drop down to a plank bridge and turn hard right at the wooden footpath signpost. After 100 yds (91m) swing left

GPS WAYPOINTS

🖊 SZ 455 985	**C** SZ 436 997
A SZ 448 985	**D** SZ 430 988
B SZ 446 996	

onto the signposted bridleway, following the enclosed trail until it bears left and joins the gravelled farm road at East Hill Farm. This attractive, tree-lined route continues between fields and brings you to the Exbury–Lepe road.

C Cross the road, and continue along the signposted footpath that follows the edge of Cump Copse on your left. At the corner of the wood, keep straight on towards the trees ahead. Turn left at a three-way footpath signpost when you reach the trees, keeping the woods on your right. Continue through a gap in the hedge, still following the woodland edge as far as a stile and three-way wooden signpost.

Go over the stile and follow the signposted path, hugging the woods on your right until a wooden signpost points your way to the right, across a waymarked wooden footbridge. Continue through a scrubby area, cross another waymarked bridge, and follow the signposted route over a third footbridge and out through a wooden kissing-gate onto a tarred lane. This section may be muddy in wet weather.

D Turn left onto the road, keeping an eye out for the occasional car. A

Grey plover on marshland

few yards farther on the Solent comes back into view and, as the road meets the shore, a wooden signpost leads you onto the foreshore footpath. *This path may flood at high tide, in which case simply follow the road back to Lepe.*

Pick your way along the foreshore past Inchmery House, where an overgrown path leads off through part of the North Solent Site of

Lepe is one of Hampshire's most popular country parks. The fresh air, wildlife and wonderful views all help to attract more than 600,000 visitors every year. The park has its own information centre, with a variety of books and leaflets to help you make the most of your visit.

Storm clouds above the Watch House, Lepe

Special Scientific Interest. This varied wildlife haven covers about eight miles of the west Solent coastline, and supports many rare plants, as well as breeding gulls, terns, waders and migratory birds.

Carry on along the beach, and soon you'll see the remains of extensive sea defences built to combat coastal erosion – but the slumped cliffs and bleached stumps of fallen pine trees bear silent testimony to the futility of man's efforts. Now the Watch House comes back into view; from here, simply continue along the beach to the lighthouse, and retrace your outward steps back to the start and your car.

Inchmery House was built around 1780 as the dower house for nearby Exbury. Lionel de Rothschild bought the building in 1912, planning to encircle it with lavish gardens – but his hopes were thwarted when he could not get permission to divert the road into Lepe. Instead, de Rothschild moved to Exbury in 1919, and founded the world famous gardens that still surround the de Rothschild family home to this day.

Around Burley

START Burbush Hill
DISTANCE 4¼ miles (6.8km)
TIME 2½ hours
PARKING Forestry Commission car park at the start
ROUTE FEATURES There's a single stile, several short steep climbs with heathland tracks and village roads. The walk may be muddy, and dogs should be led near grazing animals

13

After an easy walk along the old railway, the route climbs over the heather-clad slopes of Turf Hill to the bustling village of Burley with its inviting pubs, tearooms and souvenir shops. The walk winds through the village and over Burley Hill to end with a peaceful stroll across the lonely heaths of Kingston Great Common.

Take the waymarked exit from the far end of the car park, then follow the sandy path down onto the old railway line and bear left. The wide, double track formation slips effortlessly across the boggy heath until, at length, a short cutting heralds the massive brick remains of Greenberry Bridge, demolished in 1995.

A Turn left between the abutments, climbing briefly as the sandy track breaks out onto the open heath. Now the path drops through Holmsley Bog, passing an attractive pool on a well-made causeway. Smaller paths diverge as you begin the climb towards Turf Hill, but your way lies along the main gravel path as it heads towards the wide yellow scar on the slope ahead.

The climb ends as suddenly as it began, and it's mainly level walking as the gravel path draws closer to the road. Ignore all side turnings and continue until you reach a long, narrow car park crossing your path.

B Cross the car park and continue onto the woodland path straight

PUBLIC TRANSPORT Buses from Southampton and Ringwood (0870 608 2608)
REFRESHMENTS Choice of pubs and tearooms in Burley
PUBLIC TOILETS Adjacent to the Queen's Head, Burley
PICNIC/PLAY AREA None, but plenty of opportunities for informal picnics
ORDNANCE SURVEY MAPS Explorer OL22 (New Forest)

The old-fashioned craft of **cider making** has been revived in the heart of Burley village. Visitors to Littlemead, just off Pound Lane, can watch traditional cider apples being pressed during the annual open weekend in October (01425 403589 for details). After the juice has fermented, the cider is blended in freshly emptied whisky barrels to enhance the flavour. You can taste and buy draught cider straight from the barrels, and the shop also stocks a selection of New Forest gifts.

ahead. The path skirts additional car parking on your right, and then crosses the drive to Moorhill House Hotel. Keep ahead past a low wooden barrier, and pick your way down through the woods as the road converges from your right.

Soon you'll meet the road; cross over, and follow the pavement down past the unusual 'Rest and be thankful' marker stone. Bear left

GPS WAYPOINTS

🖉 SU 202 017		Ⓒ SU 205 034	
Ⓐ SU 218 015		Ⓓ SU 199 035	
Ⓑ SU 214 028		Ⓔ SU 197 031	

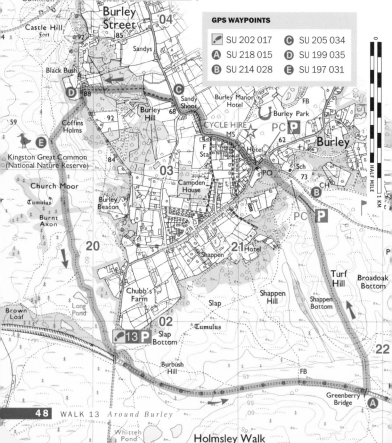

past the Queen's Head, then right at the War Memorial, signposted towards Ringwood. Follow the roadside pavement out of the village as far as Clough Lane, then cross over to a small metal gate and take the signposted footpath to Burley Street.

This tarred footway leads you safely away from the traffic to rejoin the road at a second gate. Cross over and continue along the pavement for 50 yds (46m) to the large brick gate pillars of Burley Hill House.

C Turn left, and join the signposted footpath at the wrought iron pedestrian gate to the right of the main drive. The path winds uphill between fences, crosses two footbridges, then bears left at the top of the hill to end at a stile.

D Nip across and turn left onto the gravel trackway. After 75 yds (69m), just beyond the end of the fence on your right, turn off at right angles onto a rough woodland path. The path soon breaks clear of the trees and drops down through the bracken with wide views across Kingston Great Common.

The bracken, too, soon falls behind, leaving a thin path through

Charles Castleman, a Wimborne solicitor, promoted the first railway between Southampton and Dorchester. To a walker, this section seems broad and straight, but in fact the line took a slow, roundabout route that earned it the nickname of '**Castleman's Corkscrew**'. The railway closed during the mid-1960s, but Walk 11 includes a visit to Holmsley Station, which is now a popular tearoom.

the heather. Then, at the foot of the hill, you'll reach a T-junction with a slightly wider sandy path.

E Turn left onto this path, which strikes across the heath and continues through a sandy gulley towards Burnt Axon. Keep going through the light woodland, then on across the heath until a few scatttered trees herald the end of the sandy path as you approach Long Pond on your right side.

Bear left here, through the trees, and continue along an indistinct path through the heather towards a line of electricity wires. Now the road draws closer on your left; pass beneath the power lines to meet the road opposite the car park where your walk began. ●

? *When was 'peace restored'?*

14 Beaulieu and Buckler's Hard

No guide to the New Forest would be complete without this classic walk, linking the popular centre of Beaulieu with the historic shipbuilding village of Buckler's Hard. The linear route offers easy walking, and includes a lovely waterside loop on the return. Come in spring or autumn to avoid the crowds, and to catch the seasonal colours at their best.

START Beaulieu High Street

DISTANCE 4¼ miles (6.8km)

TIME 2 hours

PARKING Pay and Display car park behind Beaulieu Garage

ROUTE FEATURES Gravel paths and a rutted woodland section with timber boardwalks; all-terrain buggies should get through. Please lead dogs in the villages

Take the gravelled footpath out of the car park, and turn left into High Street at the village shop. Turn right at the bottom of this pretty street, pass the Montagu

Palace House, Beaulieu

Arms, and turn right again into Fire Station Lane towards Buckler's Hard.

Pass the fire station, and follow the gravel track as it bends to the right. The track continues through the waymarked wicket-gate at Taylers Close, and there are attractive views across the wide river valley. A wicket-gate bypasses the cattle-grid, and you pass a small water treatment works on the left before entering the North Solent National Nature Reserve. The reserve's rich

PUBLIC TRANSPORT Buses from Lyndhurst, Lymington and Hythe (0870 608 2608)

REFRESHMENTS Beaulieu: The Old Bakehouse Tearooms and also the rather upmarket Montagu Arms. Buckler's Hard: Yachtsman's Galley and bar, also Captain's Cabin café

PUBLIC TOILETS Beaulieu and Buckler's Hard

PICNIC/PLAY AREA Waterside picnic tables and bench seats at Buckler's Hard

ORDNANCE SURVEY MAPS Explorer OL22 (New Forest)

Overlooking Beaulieu

mudflats, saltmarsh and coastal grazing are internationally important for overwintering and migratory waterfowl, and also support large numbers of breeding gulls, terns and wading birds.

The river slips away behind the trees as you enter a more intimate landscape of reedbeds, and the path winds up a short slope. There are glimpses of the river through the hedgerow trees on your left, and an open field on your right. Now the path winds past Brickyard Cottage and dives into Keeping Copse. The waymarked route zigzags right, then left, and passes a wooden barrier at the start of a long wooded section.

Ⓐ The Riverside Walk turns off to the left about 100 yds (91m) beyond the barrier. This will be

> **Beaulieu Abbey** was created on the site of a former royal hunting lodge at Bellus Locus Regis. King John specifically exempted the land from forest law when he gave it to the Cistercians in 1202. As a result, the monks could exploit the estate's timber and other resources, and the abbey gradually acquired other estates in the region. After the Dissolution, the abbey was partially demolished to provide building materials for nearby **Hurst Castle**.

your homeward route; but, for now, keep ahead down the long wooded straight until you reach a small car park on your left-hand side near the end of the woods. Just here, the gated boardwalk on the left leads to a public bird watching hide.

B Follow the waymarked track as it leaves the woods and swings to the right. There are views to Keeping Farm here, and soon you pass the Agamemnon Boat Yard on the left. Cross the boatyard access road and swing left here, following the waymarked route until it meets the river and continues along the waterfront. From here it's just a short amble past an enchanting little thatched cottage – built by the Duke of Montagu in 1760 – to the Swiftsure jetty and Buckler's Hard.

C You can easily spend a few hours at Buckler's Hard. The village was once home to workers in the nearby shipyard, and Admiral Nelson's favourite ship, *HMS Agamemnon*, was amongst over 50 Royal Navy vessels built here during the 18th and 19th centuries. The original buildings lining the village street include reconstructions of the former New Inn, as well as an 18th century labourer's cottage. Here, too,

you'll find the present-day Yachtsman's Galley and bar, whilst the Maritime Museum and other facilities are located at the top of the High Street.

To return to Beaulieu, retrace your steps to point **B** and

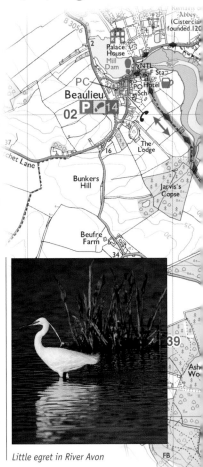

Little egret in River Avon

fork right onto the signposted Riverside Walk. The path loops off through the trees towards the river, and there are quiet spots to sit and admire the view as you follow the tree-fringed shoreline.

Wooden footbridges lead you safely across the little streams, and a curving timber boardwalk leads

The river cruiser *Swiftsure* operates regular half-hour trips from **Buckler's Hard**. As the cruiser picks its way downstream between wooded banks towards the mouth of the river, passengers might see heron, tern, little egret, and a variety of wading birds on the inter-tidal mudflats.

to a fork where two bridges diverge. Keep right here and continue beside the river until, at length, a series of long timber boardwalks herald your return to the main path.

Ⓐ Turn right, pass the wooden barrier, then zigzag right and left on the approach to Brickyard Cottage. There was once a brickworks at Bailey's Hard, and the *Salisbury* – the first naval vessel to be built on the Beaulieu River – was constructed here in 1698.

From here, simply retrace your outward steps back into Beaulieu. ●

Who was Henry Adams?

GPS WAYPOINTS

🖉 SU 386 021   **Ⓑ** SU 405 007
Ⓐ SU 396 012   **Ⓒ** SU 408 001

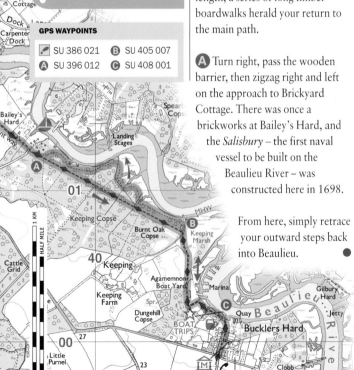

15 *Seabirds and salt at Keyhaven*

START The Gun Inn, Keyhaven

DISTANCE 4¾ miles (7.6km)

TIME 2½ hours

PARKING Keyhaven Pay and Display car park at the start. Limited free roadside parking nearby (4 hours maximum stay)

ROUTE FEATURES Level walking on country tracks and coastal paths; three stiles and short sections along minor roads

Stunning views, world class bird watching and an excellent pub distinguish this varied route. The landfill sites that once dominated the first mile have now largely been restored for wildlife and agriculture, although a few remaining contractors are still adding some finishing touches. Please lead dogs on the marshes and sea wall, to avoid disturbing waterfowl and ground nesting birds.

Turn right out of the car park, then right again up the 'no through road' beside the harbour. This is an attractive spot, with good views to Hurst Castle and the Isle of Wight. Just beyond the bridge, the Solent Way swings off along the sea wall on your right – this will be your homeward track but, for now, keep straight on. Dodge around the five-bar gate across the lane, and pass the nature reserve on the right.

A Now fork left, squeezing past a large metal gate onto the signposted footpath, and follow the unmade Iley Lane through the attractively restored landscape. The lane straightens out and heads north for an easy ¾ mile (1.2km). At length a farm track turns off to the left, and after 70 yds (64m) you'll come to a signpost and gate at the entrance to Efford recycling centre.

B Cross the access road, and continue through a gate onto the signposted footpath opposite. Soon the path goes through a metal gate,

PUBLIC TRANSPORT None

REFRESHMENTS The Gun Inn, Keyhaven and The Chequers, Woodside

PUBLIC TOILETS At the start

PICNIC/PLAY AREA None, but there are bench seats at Keyhaven for informal picnics

ORDNANCE SURVEY MAPS Explorer OL22 (New Forest)

and you continue along a tarred lane, shaded by tall hedges and young oaks, until the track ends at a second metal gate. Just beyond the gate, turn left onto a country lane.

C After 150 yds (137m), turn off over a signposted stile on your right, and follow the footpath along the right-hand field edge. Continue through a gap in the

Birdwatchers flock to **Keyhaven**, attracted by the large numbers of wading birds and other waterfowl that feed on the old salt pans and inter-tidal mudflats. Bring your binoculars and, depending on the season, you may see Brent geese, wigeon and redshank, as well as great crested grebe, little terns and common terns. The birds also roost in the surrounding marshes.

GPS WAYPOINTS

SZ 305 915	**C** SZ 317 934
A SZ 309 918	**D** SZ 322 936
B SZ 311 931	**E** SZ 318 927

hedge and along the right-hand edge of a second field. The path is soon enclosed by a fence on your left; 100 yds (91m) farther on, zigzag right and left over a stile and keep walking in the same direction, crossing two more stiles before the path ends near Meadow Cottage. Continue along the drive beside Chequers Green to join the village road at a letterbox.

D Just on your left, The Chequers makes a welcome break. To continue the walk, turn right past Chequers Green and Woodside Farm and follow the winding lane to its end at Oxey Farm House, where you continue onto the signposted footpath straight ahead. This pleasant, tree-shaded path leads between wire fences until it meets a tarred lane at an attractive, lily-fringed pond. Turn left, and follow the lane until it ends at a small parking area.

E Turn left through the pedestrian gate, then bear left down a straight gravel track banked up above the surrounding marshes. Here, in late summer, the hedge is thick with teasels and

weighed down with blackberries. The track heads straight for the coast and up onto the sea wall; turn right, and follow the sea wall path all the way back to Keyhaven.

The views from the sea wall are quite breathtaking. Hurst Castle stands out clearly in the foreground, and flotillas of small sailing craft plough the Solent in a changing panorama that stretches from Newtown to the Needles. On the landward side, large numbers of seabirds feed around the fringes of shallow lagoons – sad reminders of the salt pans that were a mainstay of the local economy until the mid-19th century.

As you meet the road, turn left through the kissing-gate to retrace your outward route over the bridge and back to your car. ●

Sea salt production was a major local industry for 700 years. At the start of the 19th century the **Lymington** area produced 6,000 tons annually, valued at a shilling (5p) a bushel. Salt was already highly taxed, but now a levy of 15 shillings (75p) a bushel was imposed to help finance the Napoleonic wars. This punitive tax added to the problems of competition from the Cheshire salt mines and, by 1845, the local industry had collapsed.

Lymington and Buckland Rings

START Lymington Town railway station
DISTANCE 4¼ miles (7km)
TIME 2½ hours
PARKING Town centre Pay and Display car park
ROUTE FEATURES A blend of town pavements, rural paths and country lanes. Please keep your dog on a lead through the Reedbeds Nature Reserve, which may be muddy after rain

16

On Saturdays this route leads straight into the thick of Hampshire's leading street market – a colourful experience, with traffic chaos to match, so box clever. Come by train, and forget the traffic as you thread your way out over the Iron Age fort at Buckland Rings, returning through a peaceful nature reserve beside the Lymington River.

🥾 Walk up Station Street and turn left at the top; then, after 150 yds (137m), bear round to the right into High Street. Here, Lymington's Saturday market rivals any in Hampshire, with colourful stalls selling everything you could wish for. Near the top of the High Street stands the town's oldest building, St Thomas's church, with its domed cupola and south tower. Inside, the substantial galleries that surround three sides of the nave are panelled with plaques recording the church's history.

Follow the path through the churchyard, and out past the fire station onto Avenue Road. Turn left here, then right at the traffic lights,

Early in the 19th century, Mrs St Ann Barbe gave £220 to buy the site '... for a school for poor children of the parish of Lymington'. The school was subsequently built in New Lane (now New Street, just off the High Street) and opened in 1836. The **Lymington Museum Trust** saved the old school building, which now houses the charming visitor centre and St Barbe Museum.

PUBLIC TRANSPORT Trains from Southampton and Brockenhurst (08457 484950)
REFRESHMENTS The Toll House Inn, Buckland, plus a wide choice in Lymington town centre
PUBLIC TOILETS In the car park
PICNIC/PLAY AREA None
ORDNANCE SURVEY MAPS Explorer OL22 (New Forest)

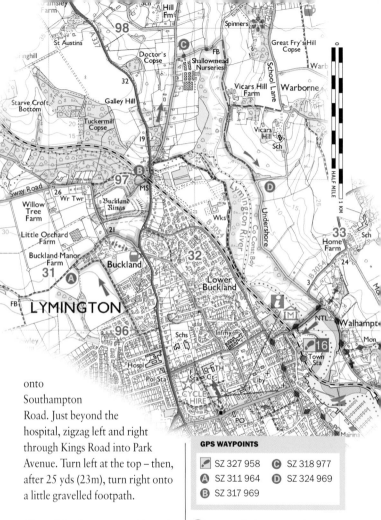

onto Southampton Road. Just beyond the hospital, zigzag left and right through Kings Road into Park Avenue. Turn left at the top – then, after 25 yds (23m), turn right onto a little gravelled footpath.

The path leads you across Alexandra Road and away from the town towards the red brick buildings of Buckland Manor Farm. The path loops left and right in front of the farm buildings, then pulls up short at a three-way footpath signpost.

GPS WAYPOINTS

🖊 SZ 327 958		**C**	SZ 318 977
A SZ 311 964		**D**	SZ 324 969
B SZ 317 969			

A Turn right here onto the gravelled track through the farmyard and out onto Sway Road. Cross the road, and nip through the wooden kissing-gate opposite.

For a diversion to the Toll House

Buckland Rings near Lymington

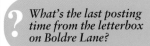

What's the last posting time from the letterbox on Boldre Lane?

Inn, follow the field edge on the right for 200 yds (182m), as far as a second gate on the right-hand side. Leave the field here, and turn left for the 100-yd (91m) walk to the pub – but do take care, as this is quite a busy road.

To continue the walk, bear left from the first gate and walk diagonally across the field towards Buckland Rings Iron Age fort. A succession of similar gates will lead you through the ancient earthworks; take the right-hand path across the centre of the fort, towards the railway bridge at the northeast corner of the site. Here, a few steps lead steeply down onto the A337.

B Cross over, and turn left under the railway. Then, immediately beyond the Ampress Park roundabout, take the right-hand fork up tree-shaded Boldre Lane and continue for ½ mile (800m).

C Just past Shallowmead Nurseries, dive off to the right down a little sunken lane, and cross the infant Lymington River by a white-railed footbridge. Fifty yards (45m) farther on, turn right through a wooden five-bar gate and follow the bridleway that leads down through the Reedbeds Nature Reserve.

D The path leaves the reserve and continues straight on along Undershore, following this quiet lane for ½ mile (800m). Keep straight ahead at the B3054 junction, staying with the road as it sweeps to the right and crosses the Lymington River. But for the traffic on the bridge, this would be a peaceful scene. Beyond the river and level crossing, turn immediately left down Waterloo Road to return to the station. ●

The 80-acre (32ha) **Reedbeds Nature Reserve** is owned by the Hampshire Wildlife Trust. Otters live in the river, and the site is home to some 300 species of moths and butterflies. Look out, too, for swallows and housemartins, as well as the rarer reed warbler and Cetti's warbler.

17 *Around Norleywood*

START Crockford Clump, 2½ (4km) miles NE of Lymington on B3054

DISTANCE 4¾ miles (7.6km)

TIME 2½ hours

PARKING Small Forestry Commission car park at the start

ROUTE FEATURES Gentle slopes and boggy places at first; then mainly level walking, interspersed with several stiles

This walk begins with a long section on indistinct heathland paths to East End. Here the route changes its character, heading south through Sowley Copse before continuing to Norleywood on country lanes and field paths. Finally, a pleasant walk through Norley Inclosure leads you back to the heath where your walk began.

Turn left out of the car park and follow the roadside verge down through the heather and gorse towards Crockford Bridge. As you drop down the hill, it's worth spending a few moments getting your bearings.

Directly in front of you, the Crockford Stream crosses the road at right angles and curves away in a little wooded valley to your left. For the first 1½ miles (2.4km), you'll be walking on barely defined tracks across the heath, following this valley as it curves southwards towards East End. You'll drop

Cottage at East End

down to cross several minor tributaries along the way, but stay within 200 yds (182m) of the Crockford Stream and you won't go very far wrong.

PUBLIC TRANSPORT Buses from Lymington and Hythe (0870 608 2608)

REFRESHMENTS The East End Arms

PUBLIC TOILETS None

PICNIC/PLAY AREA None, but plenty of pleasant spots for informal picnics

ORDNANCE SURVEY MAPS Explorer OL22 (New Forest)

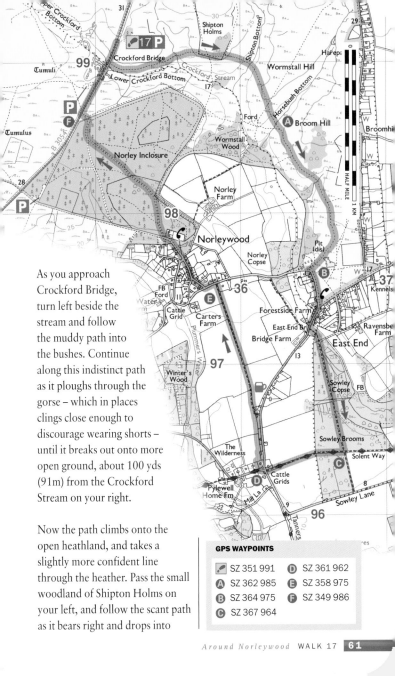

As you approach Crockford Bridge, turn left beside the stream and follow the muddy path into the bushes. Continue along this indistinct path as it ploughs through the gorse – which in places clings close enough to discourage wearing shorts – until it breaks out onto more open ground, about 100 yds (91m) from the Crockford Stream on your right.

Now the path climbs onto the open heathland, and takes a slightly more confident line through the heather. Pass the small woodland of Shipton Holms on your left, and follow the scant path as it bears right and drops into

GPS WAYPOINTS

🖊 SZ 351 991	Ⓓ SZ 361 962
Ⓐ SZ 362 985	Ⓔ SZ 358 975
Ⓑ SZ 364 975	Ⓕ SZ 349 986
Ⓒ SZ 367 964	

About a tenth of all the world's lowland heaths are found in southern England. Heather, gorse and bog myrtle thrive on the **New Forest's** acid soils, and the heaths support a characteristic variety of wildlife. Here you may see adders or grass snakes, as well as nightjar, woodlark, or even the rare Dartford warbler. Plants like sundews and bog asphodel grow in the damp valley bottoms, which are also home to dragonflies, damselflies and bush-crickets.

Shipton Bottom. Cross the brook here, and follow the sheep track out of this tiny valley, still bearing to your right as the Crockford Stream swings southwards. A track crosses your path near the summit of Wormstall Hill, and the path drops into Horsebush Bottom.

Ⓐ Cross the tiny stream, and follow the boggy track leading up from the water. After 100 yds (91m) you'll come to a drier area, with gravel underfoot, where two paths diverge. Take the right-hand fork, skirt the oak woods on Broom Hill, and drop down under the electricity wires to another little brook. Continue straight

> **?** *Who owns the noticeboard beside Norleywood bus shelter?*

ahead, ignoring a path that forks off to the right beside a clump of young oak trees. On the brow of the low hill the path bears right, picking its way across an open area of low gorse bushes, with grazing cattle and glimpses of the houses away on your left. Still veering to the right, you'll suddenly come to a lily pond on your left-hand side. Pass the pond, bear right, and after 100 yds (91m) you'll reach the thatched Sheepwash Cottage on the back lane from Norleywood.

Ⓑ Turn left onto the lane, continue down to the junction, and bear right towards Lymington and South Baddesley. Cross a little white-railed bridge, and continue for 30 yds (27m) to a signposted stile on your left. Turn left over the stile, cross a small field, and continue across a plank bridge and waymarked stile. Bear right here, cross another stile, and continue along the confident straight track through the centre of Sowley Copse. An easy ½ mile (800m) passes, and a field opens up on the left. Just here, the Solent Way crosses your path at a short wooden waymark post.

Ⓒ Turn right, and follow the Solent Way through the woods, then over a plank bridge and

Dartford warbler

the right. Pass the telephone box, and continue around the left-hand bend. Just here, a wicket gate on your right leads into Norley Inclosure. Follow the gravel track into the woods for a brisk walk through the heart of the Inclosure, until the track swings to the right, and leaves the woods at a wicket gate close to the B3054.

waymarked stile into a field. Continue along the right-hand field edge, until you meet Tanners Lane at a small wooden kissing-gate.

D Turn right, and follow the road for 400 yds (364m) towards East End and East Boldre, as far as the public footpath sign beside Briarwood Cottage on your left. *If you fancy a break, continue just a little further to the East End Arms –* otherwise, turn left over this stile. After a few paces, cross another stile and turn right, following the edge of a fruit field. Continue through a gap into a second field, and keep straight ahead onto the enclosed path that leads all the way to Norleywood.

E Cross the stile, turn left, and follow the village road around to

F Turn right, and pick your way over the heath, roughly parallel to the road. Cross Crockford Bridge – or ford the stream – for the gentle climb back to the car park. ●

Villages like **Norleywood** and **East Boldre** grew up during the 17th and 18th centuries, when cottages and small paddocks were encroaching onto the forest heaths. The owners grazed their animals on the heath, which was also a valuable source of domestic materials. Heather was used for roofing, and fern provided cheap bedding for the animals. Birch twigs were made into besoms, or simple brooms, while the ancient right of 'turbary' allowed commoners to dig peat for fuel.

18 *Around Linwood*

START Broomy Walk,
5 miles (8km) NE of
Ringwood

DISTANCE 5 miles (8km)

TIME 2½ hours

PARKING Small Forestry
Commission car park at
the start. (Alternative car
park at Spring Bushes)

ROUTE FEATURES An easy
route on forest tracks
and minor roads with an
optional short cut.
Please lead your dog
near grazing animals

After crossing a wide expanse of heather, this varied walk joins the cycle track through Broomy Inclosure. It winds on through a pastoral landscape dotted with houses, before the short climb out of the valley past the Red Shoot Inn. Bring your binoculars, because you'll often see deer along this route, which is also good for birdwatching.

🖉 Leave the car park and turn right up the roadside verge, passing the turning to the High Corner Inn on your left. About 200 yds (182m) past Spring Bushes car park, bear away left onto a grassy track that curves steadily across the plateau. There are charming views across the open heather landscape, which is studded with small trees and patches of woodland, and it's a good place to see Dartford warbler, meadow pipit and stonechat. After ½ mile (800m) of pleasant, easy walking, the path meets a waymarked cycle track at an oblique 'crossroads'.

Ⓐ Continue straight ahead onto this wide, well-made gravel track. Fallow deer are visible anywhere on this walk, especially early in the morning or at dusk. You'll often see them here in Broomy Bottom, off to your right as you wind down past the trees surrounding Broomy Lodge. The track drops into Broomy Inclosure at the gate to Holly Hatch Cottage: keep straight on, and continue for 300 yds (273m) to a wooden cycle track waymark at the forest crossroads.

PUBLIC TRANSPORT None

REFRESHMENTS Red Shoot Inn, Linwood; also diversion to the High Corner Inn

PUBLIC TOILETS None

PICNIC/PLAY AREA None

ORDNANCE SURVEY MAPS Explorer OL22 (New Forest)

What are the conditions for walking in Broomy and Holly Hatch Inclosures?

Ⓑ Turn left along the lovely tree-shaded track with its soft green verges. You can see all three species of woodpecker in these woods, as well as wood warbler, redstart, blackcap and many others. As you follow the waymarked route through a wooden gate into a conifer plantation, look out for coal tits and goldcrest, too.

Gradually, the trees revert to a mixture of oak and beech and, at length, the track leaves Broomy Inclosure at a second wooden gate. Continue straight on as the woods fall light through timbered parkland: after heavy rain, you may see dragonflies over the small pools bordering the track here.

Fungi are plentiful in the woods, especially in autumn. Look out for beefsteak fungus on the oaks, as well as porcelain fungus on rotting beech trees and fallen branches. **Fly agaric**, familiar in children's books for its distinctive red cap and white spots, can often be seen on the forest floor. *Do not forget, though, that this attractive toadstool is poisonous.*

Dockens Water ford, Woodford Bottom

Now, just beyond a wooden barrier, the track comes to a T-junction.

C *The High Corner Inn lies a ¼ mile (402m) to your left here – and, if time is pressing, you can short-circuit the walk by continuing past the pub and back to your car.* Otherwise, turn right, and follow the track past a shallow ford of the Dockens Water on your right. Keep an eye out for roe deer in the cultivated fields between here and point **D** at around sunset; they are our smallest native species and, unlike fallow deer, they never have spots on their coats.

GPS WAYPOINTS

🖊 SU 197 099		**C**	SU 195 111
A SU 209 109		**D**	SU 183 098
B SU 213 116			

During the 3rd and 4th centuries, this little valley would have been dotted with small kilns, serving the demand for locally produced pottery throughout this part of Roman Britain. The potters were largely itinerant craftsmen, who set up their works close to supplies of clay, sand, water and fuel. They built circular kilns, and their imitations of the popular Samian and Rhenish designs would have

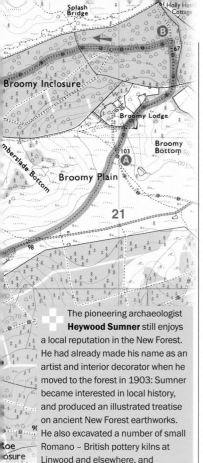

been distributed on the newly built network of Roman roads.

Now the cycle track winds through an area of scattered houses and rough grazing, and past the low, tree-capped mound of Black Barrow. In this area, and in the fields near point **D**, you may occasionally see red deer, our largest native species. Pass Little Pointers Farm on your left, and continue across the open heath to the picturesque thatched Bogmyrtle Cottage, where another track swings in from your left. Keep walking straight ahead, following the waymarked cycle track out onto a tarred lane. Soon, the lane swings left over a ford, where the small footbridge is a blessing in wet weather.

D The lane climbs steadily to the Red Shoot Inn. Muddy boots, children and dogs are all welcome in this friendly old pub, where you can sample beer brewed on the premises.

Bear left onto the rough track past the front of the pub, onto the road leading up from Appleslade Bottom. *This road can be busy, so do watch out for traffic.*

Cross over and turn left, picking your way through Lin Wood a few yards from the road as you climb towards Amie's Corner. Cross the turning to Roe Cottage and continue through the woods until you reach a track, parallel with the road, that will lead you back to your car. ●

19 *Around the Islands*

This splendid route makes a complete circuit of Islands Thorns Inclosure. After a glorious crossing of The Butts, with open views over Leaden Hall and Ashley Hole, you'll swing east through the woods and climb gently to a refreshment stop at Fritham. A further woodland stretch brings you out onto Homy Ridge for a heathland finale.

START Telegraph Hill, near the junction of B3078 and B3080
DISTANCE 5½ miles (8.7km)
TIME 3 hours
PARKING Small Forestry Commission car park at the start
ROUTE FEATURES Mainly easy walking on heathland and forest tracks. There are some moderate slopes, as well as a rather damp, indistinct path through Eyeworth Wood

Turn left out of the car park and, after 20 yds (18m), turn left again at the low wooden barrier directly opposite Hope Cottage. Your route follows the gravel track across a wide, level heath, marred only by the noise of traffic and a distant line of electricity pylons.

The track bears left soon after you've passed a small, seasonal pond on your right at Studley Head. Then, 250 yds (228m) farther on, it dives briefly beneath holly and oak trees before breaking back out onto the heath. The traffic noise dies away, and the pylons slip behind you.

Grey squirrel, near Ringwood

PUBLIC TRANSPORT Infrequent service from Southampton to Fritham (0870 608 2608)
REFRESHMENTS The Royal Oak, Fritham
PUBLIC TOILETS None
PICNIC/PLAY AREA None, but plenty of informal picnic spots
ORDNANCE SURVEY MAPS Explorer OL22 (New Forest)

A Continue past a deep, squarish pool on your right, itself just a few paces beyond the low mound of a tumulus. The track winds between a few scattered trees, and passes a second pool on the right. During the Second World War, the Ashley Walk bombing range encompassed some 4,000 acres (1618 ha) of heathland away to your right. Inside its 9-mile (14km) perimeter fence, the site was a maze of natural and man-made targets that included bunkers, trenches and steel plates, as well as

two massive concrete walls at Cockley Plain and Leaden Hall.

GPS WAYPOINTS

🖉	SU 228 166	**D**	SU 227 145
A	SU 213 156	**E**	SU 229 157
B	SU 208 141	**F**	SU 230 160
C	SU 231 141		

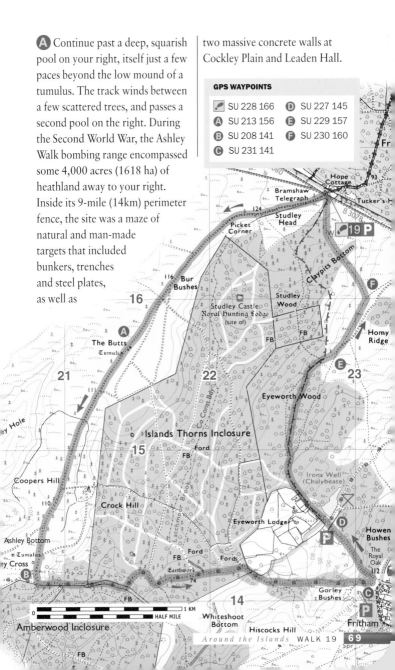

The range was a test bed for a wide variety of military hardware, including the largest bomb ever to be dropped in England – the 22,000-lb 'Grand Slam' designed by Sir Barnes Wallis. Another of his creations, the famous 'Dam Buster' bouncing bomb, was also tested here. During the mid-1970s, one of these bombs was reconstructed out of sections salvaged from Ashley Walk, and presented to the RAF's 617 'Dam Buster' Squadron. Sir Barnes Wallis himself attended the ceremony, which was held at Middle Wallop air base, near Andover.

More than 400 craters were counted on aerial photographs taken after the range closed in 1946, but half a century later there's little left to see. Just follow the track south towards Amberwood Inclosure, ignoring the path that branches off around the edge of Ashley Bottom to your right. A little farther on, the small brick and concrete hut on your right is the only wartime building left on the former Ashley Walk range.

B The long march over the heath ends at a waymarked junction with the cycle track on the edge of Amberwood Inclosure. Turn left, and dive steeply down the well-made gravel track into the woods. Ignore any turnings, and follow the waymarked route through the forest and across the Latchmoor Brook. Gradually, the trees drop behind as the cycle track winds its way up through Gorley Bushes, and there are glimpses of Eyeworth Lodge off to your left. A steady pull brings you up to the green at Fritham. The cycle track ends at a wooden barrier, just across the green from The Royal Oak, where you can take a well-earned break in one of the New Forest's best known pubs.

C Turn left here – but, before you drop down the tarred lane towards Eyeworth Lodge, look out for the small black painted letterbox on the corner. It was erected by the nearby Schultze Gunpowder Factory in the late-19th century, and has now been renovated by the

See how many native trees you can spot in **Amberwood** and **Islands Thorns Inclosures**. Besides oak, holly, beech and yew, I noticed rowan, silver birch, whitebeam and crab apple. You'll also see Scots pine; these stately conifers are native to Scotland, but have been re-introduced into southern England. Piles of logs are often stacked in these woods, and you can tell their age by counting the rings at the end – one for each year of the tree's life.

? *What is the maximum safe clearance under the electricity wires in Gorley Bushes?*

Forestry Commission. The postman delivered and collected on six days every week, and the letterbox saved him a round trip of ½ mile (800m), to the factory at the bottom of the hill.

D Continue straight ahead at the foot of the hill, leaving Eyeworth Pond with its water lilies on your right. A short gravel track leads you up to a low wooden barrier at Oaktree Cottage: leave the barrier on your left, and take the narrow path that leads off through the trees. Go quietly here, and you may see deer grazing, especially around dawn or dusk. The path varies in character as it slips shyly through Eyeworth Wood – narrow and sandy in places, it's also broad and boggy at times.

E At length, the path leads out onto a tree-studded heath. This is firmer, more confident walking. The B3078 tracks across the woods on the horizon, and you can just make out your destination near Hope Cottage away in the distance to the left. Continue on to Homy Ridge, as far as a stocky Scots pine tree at the edge of a small wood on your right.

F The path divides here. Take the left-hand fork to return to your car, on the far side of this delightful shallow valley. ●

Pathway through Eyeworth Wood, near Fritham

20 *Ashurst to Beaulieu Road*

This elongated route loops around the railway south of Ashurst. Beginning with wooded inclosures, you'll continue through boggy Fulliford Passage and across the heath to the pony saleyard near Beaulieu Road Station. There's a similar mix of scenery on your return, and along the way you may see deer, green woodpecker, orchids or cotton grass.

START Ashurst (New Forest) railway station
DISTANCE 5½ miles (8.9km)
TIME 3 hours
PARKING Small station car park behind the New Forest Inn. Also parking over bridge, next to the Happy Cheese pub
ROUTE FEATURES Gravel tracks and forest paths; can be boggy in places. Please lead dogs through Ashurst campsite

Leave Ashurst station by the gravel path at the end of platform two, signposted 'way out to Ashurst village'. Beyond the wooden pedestrian gate turn right, then double back through a second gate into a narrow field of close-cropped turf fringed with trees and bushes.

Continue for almost ½ mile (800m), crossing a couple of small plank bridges, and staying close to the woods on your left as they bear gently away from the railway. Here you'll come to a set of wooden gates leading onto the gravelled cycle track straight ahead.

A Carry on through the gates, and follow the track into the dense mixed woodland. Turn right at the T-junction after 250 yds (229m), then continue along this waymarked route. At length the track bends around to the left, and climbs to a wooden waymark post by a pair of gates on your right.

B Go through the gates and bear right – then, just before the post

PUBLIC TRANSPORT Trains to Ashurst (New Forest) Station (08457 48 49 50)
REFRESHMENTS Ashurst: The Happy Cheese and The New Forest Inn. Beaulieu Road: The Beaulieu Road Inn
PUBLIC TOILETS None
PICNIC/PLAY AREA None, but plenty of attractive spots for informal picnics along the route
ORDNANCE SURVEY MAPS Explorer OL22 (New Forest)

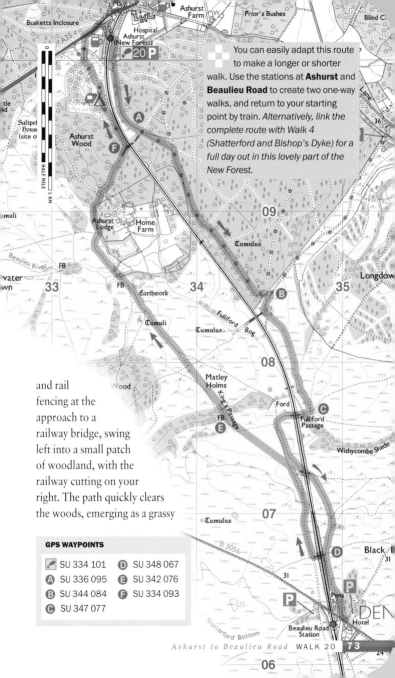

You can easily adapt this route to make a longer or shorter walk. Use the stations at **Ashurst** and **Beaulieu Road** to create two one-way walks, and return to your starting point by train. *Alternatively, link the complete route with Walk 4 (Shatterford and Bishop's Dyke) for a full day out in this lovely part of the New Forest.*

and rail fencing at the approach to a railway bridge, swing left into a small patch of woodland, with the railway cutting on your right. The path quickly clears the woods, emerging as a grassy

GPS WAYPOINTS

🖊 SU 334 101	Ⓓ SU 348 067
Ⓐ SU 336 095	Ⓔ SU 342 076
Ⓑ SU 344 084	Ⓕ SU 334 093
Ⓒ SU 347 077	

Ponies at Black Down

track across the scrubby heathland, about 100 yds (91m) from the tree-lined railway boundary.

You'll come to a boggy area near the foot of the slope, but the tussocky grass is often firm enough to carry you across dry shod. Now the path draws closer to the railway, and dodges through a gap in the hedge in front of you. Cross the trickle of water here, and follow the path as it veers towards a clump of Scots pine trees on your right.

C Turn right here, cross a wooden-railed footbridge, and dive through the railway arch straight ahead. The path quickly snakes out onto a large grazed area to your left. Bear left, and walk parallel with the railway for some 300 yds (273m) before re-crossing the line beneath an iron girder bridge. Bear

right after the bridge, following the path past a clump of large Scots pine trees nestling in a hollow of the low hill.

D Beyond the trees, you'll pass a small bridge over the railway: from here, you can see the chimneys of Fawley oil refinery on your left. *The return route swings right over this bridge, or you can continue past the pony saleyard to the Beaulieu Road Inn.*

Retrace your steps from the pub to point **C**, and turn left across the railway bridge. Turn right onto the sandy track beyond the bridge, and follow it down beside the railway to the girder bridge that you walked under on your outward

The New Forest Livestock Society's saleyard at **Beaulieu Road** is used by the Commoners to sell their ponies by auction, and is one of the safest and most efficient yards in the country. The saleyard was constructed during 2002 to replace the one that was built here just after the Second World War, and the new design was closely based on the original yard.

> **What's the weight limit on the railway bridge at point ⓒ?**

journey. Turn half-left here, and strike out diagonally across the greensward. As you approach the woods, you'll see a wooden-railed footbridge tucked into an opening about halfway along the northern side of the open field.

ⓔ Go through here, crossing the two wooden footbridges at King's Passage. As you emerge on the far side, a narrow path bears away to the right. Steer across the grass to the left of this path, aiming for the right-hand end of the gap in the woods on the skyline. As you climb the low rise, the woods blend into an unbroken vista, and you'll see a sandy track snaking through the heather straight ahead.

Continue onto this track, which carries you briskly over a low summit, past a Bronze Age earthwork and across a wide, wooden-railed footbridge. Now the track snakes right and left to meet the wooden boundary fence of Ashurst Lodge, and runs beside it as far as the low wooden barriers marking the Lodge drive. Cross over, and continue through the woods until you reach the white-

railed approach to another railway bridge.

ⓕ Turn left onto a narrower gravel path immediately before the start of the railings. Continue over a plank bridge, and follow the path as it turns left beside the railway. About 100 yds (91m) farther on, the waymarked path enters the Forestry Commission's Ashurst campsite. Follow the gravelled route to the right of the shower block, and out onto the tarmac camp access road. Keep right as the two carriageways divide; then, just past the wooden reception hut, turn off onto a grassy path on your right.

Continue over a plank bridge and out over a stile onto the A35. Turn right, and follow the roadside pavement back to your car. ●

Silver-studded blue butterfly

Further Information

Walking Safety

Always take with you both warm and waterproof clothing and sufficient food and drink. Wear suitable footwear, such as strong walking boots or shoes that give a good grip over stony ground, on slippery slopes and in muddy conditions. Try to obtain a local weather forecast and bear it in mind before you start. Do not be afraid to abandon your proposed route and return to your starting point in the event of a sudden and unexpected deterioration in the weather.

Ancient pollarded beech tree, Vinney Ridge

All the walks described in this book will be safe to do, given due care and respect, even during the winter. Indeed, a crisp, fine winter day often provides perfect walking conditions, with firm ground underfoot and a clarity of light unique to that time of the year.

The most difficult hazard likely to be encountered is mud, especially when walking along woodland and field paths, farm tracks and bridleways – the latter in particular can often get churned up by cyclists and horses. In summer, an additional difficulty may be narrow and overgrown paths, particularly along the edges of cultivated fields. Neither should constitute a major problem provided that the appropriate footwear is worn.

Global Positioning System (GPS)

What is GPS?

Global Positioning System, or GPS for short, is a fully-functional navigation system that uses a network of satellites to calculate positions, which are then transmitted to hand-held receivers. By measuring the time it takes a signal to reach the receiver, the

Shaggy pholiota

navigation on land, sea and air around the world, as well as an important tool for map-making and land surveying.

Follow the Countryside Code
- Be safe – plan ahead and follow any signs
- Leave gates and property as you find them
- Protect plants and animals, and take your litter home
- Keep dogs under close control
- Consider other people

(Natural England)

distance from the satellite can be estimated. Repeat this with several satellites and the receiver can then triangulate its position, in effect telling the reciever exactly where you are, in any weather, day or night, anywhere on Earth.

GPS information, in the form of grid reference data, is increasingly being used in Jarrold guidebooks, and many readers find the positional accuracy GPS affords a reassurance, although its greatest benefit comes when you are walking in remote, open countryside or through forests.

GPS has become a vital global utility, indispensable for modern

Useful Organisations

Campaign to Protect Rural England
128 Southwark Street, London
SE1 0SW.
Tel. 020 7981 2800
www.cpre.org.uk

English Heritage
Customer Services,
PO Box 569, Swindon
SN2 2YP.
Tel. 0870 333 1181
www.english-heritage.org.uk

National Trust
Membership and general enquiries:
PO Box 39,
Warrington
WA5 7WD.

Tel. 0870 458 4000
www.nationaltrust.org.uk

Natural England
1 East Parade, Sheffield S1 2ET.
Tel. 01142 418920
www.naturalengland.org.uk

Ordnance Survey
Romsey Road, Southampton
SO16 4GU.
Tel. 08456 05 05 05 (Lo-call)
www.ordnancesurvey.co.uk

Ramblers' Association
2nd Floor, Camelford House,
87-90 Albert Embankment,
London SE1 7TW.
Tel. 020 7339 8500
www.ramblers.org.uk

**Royal Society for the Protection
of Birds**
The Lodge, Sandy,
Bedfordshire SG19 2DL.
Tel. 01767 680551
www.rspb.org.uk

The Woodland Trust,
Autumn Park, Dysart Road,
Grantham, Lincs NG31 6LL.
Tel. 01476 581135
www.woodland-trust.org.uk

Youth Hostels Association
Trevelyan House,
Dimple Road, Matlock,
Derbyshire
DE4 3YH.
Tel. 01629 592 600
www.yha.org.uk

Footbridge over the Lymington River

Local Organisations

Forestry Commission
The Queen's House,
Lyndhurst, Hants
SO43 7NH.
Tel. 023 8028 3141
www.forestry.gov.uk

Hampshire County Council
Recreation and Heritage Dept,
Mottisfont Court, High Street,
Winchester, Hants
SO23 8ZF.
Tel. 01962 846045
www.hants.gov.uk

**Hampshire & Isle of Wight
Wildlife Trust**
Beechcroft House,
Vicarage Lane, Curdridge,
Hants SO32 2DP.
Tel. 01489 774 400
www.hwt.org.uk

Natural England
Hampshire & Isle of Wight Team,
1 Southampton Road,
Lyndhurst, Hants
SO43 7BU.
Tel. 023 8028 6410

New Forest District Council
Appletree Court, Lyndhurst,
Hants SO43 7PA.
Tel. 023 8028 5000
www.nfdc.gov.uk

New Forest National Park
South Efford House, Milford
Road, Everton, Lymington
SO41 0JD.
Tel. 01509 646000
www.newforestnpa.gov.uk

For further information on places
to visit contact:
**New Forest Visitor
Information Centre**
The Main Car Park, Lyndhurst,
Hants SO43 7NY.
Tel. 023 8028 2269
www.thenewforest.co.uk

Local Tourist Information Centres

Fordingbridge
Tel. 01425 654560
Lymington
Tel. 01590 689000
Lyndhurst
Tel. 023 8028 2269
Ringwood
Tel. 01425 470896
Southampton
Tel. 023 8083 3333

Public Transport

For all public transport enquiries
ring **Traveline** on:
Tel. 0870 608 2608
www.traveline.org.uk

Solent Blue Line Buses
Freepost, SO3313,

Eastleigh SO50 6UA.
Tel. 023 8061 8233
www.solentblueline.com

Wilts and Dorset Bus Company
Bus Station, Dolphin Centre,
Poole BH15 1SN.
Tel. 01202 673555/01722 336855
(Salisbury)
www.wdbus.co.uk

Ordnance Survey Maps
Explorer
OL22 (New Forest)

Answers to Questions
Walk 1: The cross was erected on 14 April 1944, and services were held here until D-Day (6 June 1944).
Walk 2: The Honourable Lady Hulse laid the stone on 8 August, 1924.
Walk 3: The stone takes its name from the King's surname, which was Rufus.
Walk 4: The photo shows an area of bog at Shatterford.
Walk 5: 'Hatchets' were gateways used by the commoners' animals to reach the forest for grazing.
Walk 6: Charges were one old penny a letter, and a halfpenny for newspapers. There were 240 old pence to the pound.
Walk 7: www.hwt.org.uk
Walk 8: The lakes were originally

gravel pits, which have now been landscaped and returned to nature. Sailing, fishing and water sports are also available.
Walk 9: It was erected by public subscription to commemorate Queen Victoria's Golden Jubilee in 1887.
Walk 10: Paul Wilson.
Walk 11: The Inclosure contained 500 acres (200 ha). It was enclosed in1775 and 1809, thrown open in 1846, and re-enclosed in 1896.
Walk 12: For many years this was the coastguard lookout station, ideally placed to see boats entering or leaving the Beaulieu River.
Walk 13: 27 March 1802 – probably a reference to the Treaty of Amiens, which marked the start of a 14-month break in the Napoleonic Wars.
Walk 14: Henry Adams was the Navy Board's 'resident overseer' at Buckler's Hard during the second half of the 18th century.
Walk 15: Lymington and Pennington Town Council.
Walk 16: 5:15pm, Monday to Friday.
Walk 17: Boldre Parish Council.
Walk 18: You can use the track for 'peaceful enjoyment of air and exercise', but it is not a public right of way.
Walk 19: 4.8 metres.
Walk 20: 3 tons.